THE SECRET LANGUAGE OF

Knitters

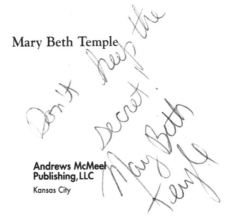

Mary Beth Temple

Don't keep the secret!
Mary Beth Temple

Andrews McMeel
Publishing, LLC
Kansas City

Acknowledgments

I ran out of room so to be brief, for once, thanks to: agent extraordinaire Kate Epstein, editor Katie Anderson, daughter Katie Temple (notice a theme here?), and all of the addicted knitters who turned a hobby into a community. Sincerely, you all rock.

07 08 09 10 11 RR2 10 9 8 7 6 5 4 3 2 1

ISBN-13: 978-0-7407-6873-6
ISBN-10: 0-7407-6873-5

Library of Congress Control Number: 2007924485

www.andrewsmcmeel.com

ATTENTION: SCHOOLS AND BUSINESSES
Andrews McMeel books are available at quantity discounts with bulk purchase for educational, business, or sales promotional use. For information, please write to: Special Sales Department, Andrews McMeel Publishing, LLC, 4520 Main Street, Kansas City, Missouri 64111.

Introduction

Y ou knew there was a secret language of knitters, didn't you? You followed the "open" sign of a local yarn store like a foundering sailor following the beacon of a lighthouse, only to discover that once you found what should be your spiritual home, you didn't understand half of the words or any of the jokes. People were laughing about having tons of UFOs—had you stumbled into a sci-fi convention by mistake? They were talking about SABLE (fur?) and SEX— well, you knew what that was but why were groups of knitting women and men talking about doing it as a group right out loud in front of everybody? What kind of cult is this, after all? Perhaps you ran screaming into the night—but something (perhaps the cashmere) keeps drawing you back.

I present to you your field guide to the secret language of knitters. Because unlike many other groups that have been studied by outsiders (gorillas come to mind), we actually want you to join us. We want you to learn our language and become one of us. We want to welcome you with open arms, to convert you to our way of life. OK, maybe it is a little cult-like after all, but I mean that in the best possible sense. You can go anywhere in the country, find a yarn shop, and be instantly at home. And now you, too, can laugh at the jokes.

ACRYLIC *noun*: Otherwise known as fiber not found in nature. Talking about acrylic yarn with knitters is one of those things that is bound to get you into trouble whether in real life or on the Internet. Acrylic yarn has its crazed proponents and its die-hard haters. Like with many other things, I personally advocate moderation.

Back in the dawn of time, when I was learning to **knit**, there was pretty much acrylic, lumpy cotton rug yarn, or scratchy **wool**. We bought our acrylic yarn at the local dime store—it came in one-ounce or four-ounce skeins. I used to spend my allowance on one-ounce skeins of Red Heart, little knowing that I was already sliding down the slippery slope to stash acquisition. My mother and sisters would feed my habit, passing me their leftovers and the odd **skein** found in a sale bin. I happily made patchwork doll blankets out of all of the different colors.

Eventually, the college years came, and I began to indulge in a little **SEX**. I lived in New York City where there were **LYSs** in every part of town. I went through a long period where I thought that under no circumstances would I ever knit with 100 percent acrylic yarn ever again. Ever, ever, ever. Why spend hours on something made of crappy yarn? Why not get the finest fiber there is for every glorious item that slips off of my needles? Who really objects to hand washing? And then I had a child. Hand washing? I was barely washing myself. And I had to buy diapers; there was no **merino** money in the budget. Thankfully, times had changed—technology has improved yarns as well as other things, and there were some not-bad feeling acrylic yarns on the market. So I got over my prejudices. There are many other fibers I prefer, but when my then-seven-year-old wanted a blanket for her bed in neon colors, you bet I went with "throw it in the washer and the dryer" acrylic, rather than "hand wash this monster and hope it dries before mold sets in" **alpaca**.

So in the spirit of fiber moderation, I offer you the pros and cons of acrylic yarns.

Cons: It can be scratchy, it can pill with use, and it resists the magic of **blocking** in a big way. There is nothing at all natural about it, and because it can't breathe, neither can your skin when you are wearing it, so if you are at all prone to being a little, shall we say, sweaty, this is probably not your yarn of choice. It doesn't **felt**.

Pros: Price. Acrylic yarn is cheapity, cheap, cheap, cheap, and you get a lot of yardage for your dollar. It is machine washable and dryable, and no one is allergic to it. It comes in every color of the rainbow, as well as several that look like the design team was having an acid flashback, which can be kind of fun. It doesn't felt.

Like with any other product under the sun, there is bad acrylic yarn and better acrylic yarn. So let's all make a deal. I won't call all acrylic yarn cheap garbage, and you won't mock me for wearing a sweater whose costs might have equaled a car payment. I will knit some acrylic items for kids and allergic friends without grimacing, and you can maybe felt an item once in a while for fun.

It isn't acrylic yarn that is the enemy; it is badly made yarn of any fiber. Let's unite and stomp out that!

ADDICT, KNITTING *noun*: I find it very interesting that many words knitters use to describe their hobby have somehow migrated from the language of the illegal drug trade. **Stash**, needles, **dealer**, habit, addiction—like knitting is a guilty secret. Next thing you know there will be a twelve-step program: "Hello my name is Mary Beth, and I am addicted to **alpaca**." "All together now, 'Hi, Mary Beth.'"

I could quit any time—really, I could. I don't have to get my warm fuzzies by feeling all that woolly (or cottony, or lineny, or llama-y) goodness flow through my fingers. I really don't have to spend my weekends at **sheep and wool festivals**, plan my vacations around visits to cool yarn stores across the country, or have three projects going at the same time so that there is always something to do. I could learn to watch a **television** program

without doing anything else at the same time,
read about people in need without being driven to
knit each of them a hat, and spend time on the
Internet without cruising for yarn sales. I could
read, nay even write a **blog** about, I don't know,
politics, or gardening, or home improvement.

I could do any of these things, but I won't. I
love to knit, I love the process of knitting, and I
love the **finished objects** that I turn out. I love
wearing hand-knit goodies, giving them as gifts to
people I love, and sending them off to strangers
who might need them. There is a reason that
there isn't a twelve-step program for knitters, and
that reason is none of us wants to quit!

ALPACA *noun*: Alpacas are members of the
camelid family of mammals and are primarily
raised in South America, although there are a
growing number of herds in the United States.
Not only do they produce a wonderfully soft, long
staple fiber, but they are just cuter than all get-
out—much more cuddly looking than sheep—
plus, they hum! Alpaca yarn is warm and soft and
makes me want to **knit** all day (thus my online
name—Alpaca Addict).

ANGORA *noun*: I don't know who was in charge of all of this fiber-naming stuff, but whoever it was liked to mess with knitters. You might think that angora yarn comes from Angora goats, but you would be wrong. **Mohair** yarn comes from Angora goats; angora yarn comes from Angora rabbits. At my house, angora yarn comes from Cameron T. Bunny, if he happens to be in the mood to be plucked, and then I happen to feel like **spinning**. One hundred percent angora yarn is both expensive and a little bit difficult to work with because, much like Cameron, it has a tendency to shed. But find a yarn that is a blend of angora and some other soft fiber, like **merino wool**, and you will have a soft yarn that makes a fabric with a bit of fuzziness and a nice drape.

ARGYLE *noun*: If diamonds are a girl's best friend, argyle might be her favorite knitting pattern. Argyle is an **intarsia** pattern with a solid-colored background and patterns of interlocking diamonds in at least one other color.

Every decade or so, some clever **designer** decides this type of pattern—forever immortalized as the sweater pattern of choice of golfers in the 1920s—needs to be updated. There is a very clever pattern out there now in which a skull and crossbones has been added to the larger diamond and the pattern name changed to Arrghyles. I have seen some much less successful interpretations in a 1970s pattern book in colors that made it look as if the Duke of Argyll had indulged in a few too many acid tabs. Which only goes to show that you can, in fact, wreck a classic.

AT THE END OF THE ROW *phrase*: No matter how immediate your need, this is the only time you can count on a knitter putting her knitting down and doing something else. Depending on the size of the project, at the end of the row can occur every two minutes, every twenty minutes, or after upward of two hours. Sample sentence: "Mom, at the end of the row will you get my lunch?" Beware the more impatient family member who says he is willing to wait for at the end of the row but asks fourteen times how many stitches are left. He is only paying lip service to your time-keeping system. Related term: "At the end of this pattern repeat," which loosely translates to: "If you think I am putting this down in the middle of a **lace chart**, you are insane."

BALL WINDER *noun*: Ball winders are cool little toys that turn all of your yarn into handy little **yarn cakes**. You attach the end of your yarn to a slot in the center column of the winder, which turns at an angle as you crank away. Often paired with an **umbrella swift**, these are particularly useful for yarn that comes in **hanks**.

While you can wind away on autopilot (or teach your five-year-old to do it—kids love to play with ball winders!), you may want to pay at least a bit of attention to the yarn as you wind. This is a good time to look for **knots** so that you can work around them, or to check for any wildly thick or thin spots in **handspun**.

BAMBOO *noun*: 1. Panda food. While that has nothing to do with knitting, everyone knows pandas are cute and nearing extinction, so I don't begrudge them whatever juicy bamboo shoots they can stuff in their furry little mouths. 2. Bamboo **knitting needles**. Lightweight, unlikely to annoy even the grumpiest airport luggage screener, and a godsend when working on slippery yarn because they tend to be a little grabbier than metal or plastic needles. 3. Bamboo yarn. Yummmmm, silky and soft, environmentally sound, and no critters are harmed or even annoyed in the making of it—unless the bamboo is forcibly taken from a hungry panda, but I have seen no evidence that this is the case.

BIND OFF *verb*: When you are finished with a stitch forever, you bind it off, making sure that it won't turn into a **dropped stitch** where no dropped stitch should be. The good news about binding off is that it means that you are finished with a piece. The bad news is that pretty soon you

10

are going to have to engage in some activities of the **finishing** variety.

BLACK HOLE *noun*: Scientists may continue to ponder the ways of black holes, but knitters know what they contain, if not specifically where they are located: **stitch markers**; **cable needles**; **tapestry needles**; the last known copy of an irreplaceable pattern; **DPNs**; snips and scissors; the last **skein** of yarn for several projects; the second sock, glove, or mitten; the URL for that cool pattern you didn't have time to download at the time you found it but you have dreams about now; **bobbins**; tape measures; needle gauges; crochet hooks; trial sizes of every brand of hand lotion known to mankind; chocolate wrappers; wine bottle corks; small children or the toys they must have NOW; and several household pets. Not necessarily in that order. See also **project bag**.

BLOCKING *verb*: The magic process by which the judicious application of steam or water, a few (or a million) pins, and a little bit of time makes almost all of your knitting look and fit better. Really, it's true. Unless you **knit** with **acrylic**, in which case all bets are off.

11

You can apply a small amount of water with a steamer or a spray bottle, or if your knitted pieces are somewhat the worse for wear from traveling the world jammed in a tote bag, you can wash each piece and block it while it is wet. Using blocking wires or rust-proof pins tacked into a piece of foam (or the mattress on the guest-room bed), shape the damp piece of knitting to the size it wants to be (**schematics** are very helpful here) and allow it to dry completely. Take out your pins and/or wires, and you have a neatly shaped item that is just the size you need it to be.

Not only does blocking help with garment size, blocking individual pieces before assembly makes the **finishing** process go more quickly, which is always a good thing. And the blocking process also evens out any slight variations in **gauge**, or slightly wonky stitches that might have slipped by you in the knitting process.

BLOG *noun*: Blog, as many folks know, is the shortened version of Web log, which is sort of an online diary. There are thousands and thousands of blogs on the Internet—anyone with computer access and some two-finger typing skills can start one. But, as with many other things in life, blogs are better with knitting. Knitters started blogging about **WIPs** and **FOs**. Taking pictures of fabulous yarns (often called **yarn porn**), showing off their projects, talking about **yarn substitutions** that worked or didn't, **design modifications** that worked or didn't, and needles, techniques, and **patterns**. Then they started linking to each other, meeting up in real life at **sheep and wool festivals** and at fund-raising and **charity knitting** events, generally carrying on as a group. When those who aren't attached to their broadband connections at the hip think of a knitting community, they probably think of **sit-and-knit nights** at the **LYS**. But there is a wondrous online community of knitters, too. And sometimes the two communities overlap, which can be mind bending and a lot of fun. Just now, I typed the words "knit blog" into a search engine and got back over two million hits in two-tenths of a second. There is 24/7 yarny entertainment available online for free. The mind boggles. All you have to do to be perfectly happy is to learn how to Web surf and **knit** at the same time.

BOBBIN *noun*: A holder for a smallish amount of yarn. Bobbins are used when doing color work like **Fair Isle** or **intarsia**. Since working yarns are

twisted as you go when doing color work, bobbins
are much easier to maneuver than full **skeins** of
yarn. Bobbins are readily available at the **LYS**—
although as soon as you buy them, they will
disappear, and you will wind up using everything
from binder clips to the credit cards that come in
your junk mail to a package of chewing gum to
get the job done, which will make for some very
interesting looks from non-knitting strangers
when you **KIP**. Knitters, of course, will just smile
in recognition.

BOBBLE *noun*: Bobbles are sort of 3-D embellishments. Bobbles are made by **increasing** a few
stitches, working back and forth in **short rows**,
decreasing the same number of stitches, and
working that last stitch right back into the row
where you started. There are many different ways
to make bobbles; follow the specific directions
that are included with your pattern.

Beware the bobble-making addiction, however,
as bobbles rarely look fashionable on anyone over
the age of ten. While a great way to get the hang
of **short rows**, a row with a lot of bobbles is also a
quick way to lose your mind—you **knit** and knit

and knit and knit and you are still on the same row an hour after you started!

BOYFRIEND SWEATER, CURSE OF *noun*: It was a dark and stormy night . . . well, OK, it could just as easily have been a sunny afternoon in spring. But the story always ends the same way. Some unsuspecting knitter in the throes of love goes off to the yarn store because she has found The One, and nothing will show her love for him better than the perfect hand-knit sweater. She spends hours looking at patterns for something her man would appreciate. She stares at color cards, pets all the possibilities, and finally blows her entire **yarn budget** for the year on the perfect yarn.

But it doesn't end there. No, she takes her purchases home, throws all of her other **WIPs** aside and **casts on**. She **knits** on her lunch break, during her classes, on the bus or train, while she is watching TV. In fact, she knits every waking moment that she isn't gainfully employed or with the love of her life. Why did she choose such a complicated pattern? What if she runs out of **wool** and can't match the **dye lot**? What if the sneaky sleeve measurement she took of one of his inferior, store-bought sweaters while he was in the shower isn't quite right? What if he really would have preferred baby blue over midnight blue? None of this matters, because this sweater will be knit with love. Her love will infuse every stitch, and when he receives this gift from the heart, all will be perfect.

So she stays up all night the night before she plans to bestow this magical gift, sewing **seams**, **weaving in ends**, making a little tag for the back. Bleary-eyed, she meets her man at the appointed hour. Her hair may be a little awry, she may be raccoon-eyed from lack of sleep, and probably her **socks** don't match. But none of this matters because this sweater has been knit with love. Chest pounding, she presents her gift—awestruck at the power of this moment. This sweater is everything she believes in, tied up with a ribbon. She will tell her grandchildren about this moment.

Except—he doesn't get it. He thinks it is from Kohl's, says that wool is itchy, comments that he hardly ever wears sweaters. Or worse yet, he is effusive in his praise but tosses the box to the side where you know it will get kicked under the couch where that sweater will never see the light of day again, let alone grace his manly chest. But she isn't going to say anything about how hurt she is by this treatment—he is The One; he will figure it out on his own. Weeks go by. She catches up on her sleep, yet the nightmare won't go away. If he doesn't know that her heart and soul, as well as all of her discretionary income for the next eight months, were in that box, he can't be The One after all. The bloom is off the rose. She goes back to knitting socks for her girlfriends—at least they understand all of the work and thought that goes into her gifts of love.

He doesn't get this either. Can't figure out what he did wrong, although he suspects he did something. Does it maybe have something to do with the sweater she gave him? Nah, not possible; no one would get that worked up over a sweater. It must be something else.

Sooner or later, probably sooner, the relationship ends. She knows that if he didn't understand the depths of her true feelings from the contents of that box, well, she must have been fooled earlier on into thinking he was her soulmate. Better she should figure this out now rather than later. Although she does lament the loss of the wool. Could she get the sweater back and **frog** it?

Hmmmm, Mongolian **cashmere** doesn't grow on trees, you know.

He still doesn't know what hit him, is happy the relationship is over just so he can break away from the simmering sense of unease that has been following them around. He never dates a knitter again—they are just, I don't know, a little strange.

The moral of this story is: Knitting a sweater for The (possible) One is a bit like getting married—a huge commitment that not everyone is ready for. Stick to scarves, move on to hats, ease into the sweater thing. Take your time and make sure the man you eventually knit that sweater for is truly deserving of your woolly love.

BOUCLE *noun*: A type of yarn in which one of the **plies** has loops spaced throughout. The upside? Knitting with boucle yarns produces a thick cushy fabric with a lot of depth and visual interest. The downside? Until you get used to working with it, you will stick the point of your needle into one of the loops about every thirty seconds, causing you to say all sorts of nasty things. If you are a fan of boucle fabric, you will soldier on. Just maybe do your practicing in private until you can keep your boucle-related language at a PG-13 rating.

BUTTONHOLE *noun*: 1. What you call any random hole that shows up anywhere near the front of your sweater, even if you have made a pullover, because it couldn't possibly be a **mistake**. 2. The godforsaken nightmares that no matter how hard you try will not wind up evenly spaced on the button band the first (or perhaps even the fifth) time you figure the spacing. 3. The reason for a solemn vow to eschew cardigans forever because when they finally are properly aligned, you discover that they are either too large or too small for the buttons you already bought and can't return.

CABLE *noun*: 1. (*Definition for knitters only*) Cable patterns are one of those things that impress the hell out of non-knitters but are a lot easier to learn to do than they look like they should be. Knitted cables are formed when set groups of stitches switch places. The designated stitches are moved from the left-hand needle to a **cable needle** and held in front of or behind the work, the next group of stitches is knitted from the left-hand needle, then the stitches on the cable needle are knitted and placed back into the row.

Cable patterns look like braided ropes or Celtic knots and come in almost endless variations. Just be aware when you are knitting a cabled sweater that cabled fabric has less give than fabric knitted in other stitches, so you want to make sure you choose the correct size of pattern to get the amount of **ease** that you prefer. 2. (*Definition for non-knitters who ask you how you possibly managed such a feat of knitting brilliance when clearly mad knitting skills were required*) "Oh it just requires an extra needle, a complicated **chart**, telekinetic skills, and the ability to **knit** in your sleep—cables are nothing." Be sure to assume a modest air while you are spouting this nonsense—watching films based on Jane Austen novels can help you here.

CARRY ALONG *noun*: Skinny, skinny, skinny **novelty yarns** garnished with some sort of embellishment like **eyelash** strands or beads and sequins, carry alongs are the romance novels of the knitting world—all style and no substance. You can **knit** them alone on large needles for a lacy, frothy effect, or knit them together with a plain yarn to fancy things up. They are called carry alongs because they are often paired with other yarns, yet they don't appreciably change the gauge.

22

CASHMERE *noun*: Knitting cashmere is like knitting clouds. Soft, warm, and durable, cashmere is the fine hair that comes from certain breeds of goats. While there is a growing American cashmere industry, the bulk of the cashmere knitting yarn we see today comes from fiber gathered in China and Mongolia. Why is cashmere so expensive? First off, would you want to be gathering fiber from the underbelly of a goat with uncertain personal hygiene habits who lives on a steep mountainside? I didn't think so. Production of the yarn is fairly labor intensive–not only do goats have the yummy underhairs that form cashmere, they also have coarse guard hairs that need to be removed before the fiber is spun into yarn. And of course, many of us do not have the time or travel budget to fly to Asia to purchase yarn, therefore the yarn must be flown to us, which increases the price.

Cashmere is also used in blended yarns, the theory being that using less cashmere per yard will make your **yarn budget** go that much farther. But at least once in your life, you need to spring for the good stuff, even if it's for a small project. Cashmere is as much fun to **knit** as it is to wear.

CAST ON (CO) *verb*: You have a piece of yarn in one hand and a **knitting needle** in the other. You need stitches on the knitting needle so you can **knit** something already. Casting on is the method by which you get the correct number of stitches on the needle. There are several methods of casting on, many of which are explained in a basic how-to-knit book. While you can learn an all-purpose cast on, in some instances a specific cast on will give you a better look for a specific project—check your pattern to see if any suggestions are given.

CENTER PULL BALL *noun*: A ball of yarn wound so that the working yarn comes from the center of the ball rather than from the outside. Using yarn from the outside of a ball tends to make the ball skitter across the floor, picking up every possible piece of dust, pet hair, or snack crumb in its path, or make a dash for freedom by flying out of your **project bag** and out the bus or subway doors just as you were drawing yarn for the next row. Center pull balls can be wound by hand or on a **ball winder**.

Many commercial yarns claim to come in "pull **skeins**" meaning that in theory you can pull the yarn from the center, and it will work like a center pull ball. Be aware that these claims are often somewhat optimistic—if you don't pull the exact end in the exact right direction, you will spend the next three weeks of your life trying to sort out the resulting tangles. Cutting and starting over is not an option because, well, see also **weaving in ends**.

CHARITY KNITTING *noun*: One of the coolest things about being a knitter is that you instantly become a part of the knitting community. Whether you hook up (no **crochet** pun intended) with like-minded fiber folks online or at the **sit-and-knit night** at your **LYS**, or you just strike up a conversation with the woman in front of you at the grocery store checkout line whose kids are wearing hand knits, knitters tend to gather in groups and chat.

One of the things a thriving community does is take care of its own. And with many knitters, that then turns into a burning drive to take care of everyone else, too. We *know* that knitted love is the best love there is, and we want anyone who needs some to have some. Are kids freezing in Mongolia? We will **knit** them warm sweaters and contribute to the Dulaan project. Are there kids in hospitals and shelters who are scared and in pain? We will wrap them in blankets given to Project Linus. I have knitted red scarves for foster kids, afghan squares for those who have lived through a trauma and need to feel wrapped in comfort, and untold numbers of hats for everyone from preemies to adult cancer survivors.

There has been somewhat of a backlash recently against the charity knitting movement. Naysayers proclaim that my knitted items must be of low quality or made of inferior materials, or I wouldn't want to give them away. They say that if I or another knitter post pretty pictures of finished charity items on our **blogs** and Web sites that we are needy and searching for praise, and if we really wanted to do good, we would keep quiet about it. They say the recipients don't want our knitted items, and why can't we just write checks like normal people?

To these people I say: Step back quietly from the crazy lady with the pointed sticks and mind your own business. Any sort of charitable giving is intensely personal, and there is no right or wrong way to go about it. I say that it isn't your job to judge how I give back to my community, just as it isn't my job to judge your charitable works or lack thereof. I say that checks are great, but knitting is love, and people who are having a tough time in their lives need not only food and water but to know that someone somewhere cares about them and wants to offer a personal expression of that caring.

I say never underestimate the power or the desire of a knitter to do good.

CHART *noun*: Charts are a visual representation of the pattern you are working on. Whether they are color charts showing when to change yarns in **intarsia** or stitch charts indicating when to cross a **cable** or where to place the **yarn over** in a **lace** pattern, charts show succinctly what would take many paragraphs of written directions to explain.

Many new knitters are afraid of charts, but color charts aren't too scary—you see ten red squares followed by ten blue squares, and you **knit** ten red stitches followed by ten blue stitches, which is pretty intuitive. Symbol charts for cables and lace, however, tend to look to the uninitiated like what the cartoonist puts in the word balloons to represent cursing, which, depending on your choice of language when frustrated, may be terribly apropos.

27

But reading charts does get less frustrating with practice, and learning to read them doesn't really take more time than it did to learn any other sort of pattern abbreviation. The time spent is well worth it in terms of less frustration per hour in your knitting time.

CIRCULAR NEEDLES *noun*: See **needles, circular**.

COLORWAY *noun*: It just means color.

COMBINATION KNITTING *noun*: Or "Do you want plies with that?" Combination knitters combine aspects of both **Continental** and **English knitting**. In the olden days, much like schoolteachers tried to force left-handed children to write with their right hands, many knitting teachers thought combination knitters were just doing it wrong and tried to force them into the Continental or English folds. Today, there are many combination knitters who are sticking to their technical guns with pride. Be aware that most commercial patterns are written without the combination knitter in mind, and you might have to rethink some of the instructions (left- and right-leaning **decreases**, for example) to get the results you want.

CONTINENTAL KNITTING *noun*: The Continental knitter holds the working yarn in her left hand and "picks" it to create her stitches—her hands never leave the needles. Continental knitting has a reputation for being the speediest. But doesn't that term sound like it should refer to something a lot more glamorous? I hear "Continental knitting," and I think Fred Astaire and Ginger Rogers doing crafts on a transcontinental cruise. Which may, of course, only mean that I watch way too many period movie musicals.

CROCHET *verb*: That other craft with yarn. No, really, crochet is a wonderful craft that also makes fabric out of yarn, although crocheters use a hook rather than two or more needles. For some reason, and I honestly don't know what started it, there seems to be a little friction between the crochet camp and the knitting camp. I cheerfully admit in public to liking to do both, but in some places that's like saying you are a vegetarian with a predilection for cheeseburgers—a statement that is not likely to make you popular on either side of the divide.

Knitters say that crocheters only use **acrylic** yarn that sells for a dollar a ton and spend too much time making toilet paper covers shaped like fashion-challenged southern belles. Crocheters say that knitters are snobs and spend way too much money on yarn. Like all generalizations, there may be elements of truth in these statements, but taking them at face value is unlikely to make the divide any smaller. And I would like it to be smaller. Knitters and crocheters both are forces for positive change—imagine what we could accomplish if we all worked together!

Crocheted fabric as well as knitted fabric has its pros and cons. Knitted fabric can be drapier, which is nice for sweaters. Crocheted fabric holds its shape better, which is cool for structural items and embellishments. Knitted **socks** fit into your shoes more easily, yet thicker crocheted socks work up more quickly and can last longer. Crocheted fabric uses up more yarn per square inch than knitting, but it also has a tendency to go faster, which is good for us instant gratification types. Both make excellent **lace**.

My proposal to the fiber world is that we all become bi-craftual and use whatever skill is the most appropriate for the end results we are seeking. At the very least, I wish knitters would be nicer to crocheters. It makes sense on a lot of levels including this one: Crocheters outnumber knitters almost three to one. Their sticks may not be as pointy, but with the amount of yarn they have in their **stashes**, they could tie us up pretty good.

DEALER *noun*: Head honcho at your **LYS**. The dealer stays awake at night wondering how to encourage you to feed your yarn jones—what yarns will she introduce you to, which books will make you break out in a cold sweat when you see them, what classes does she want to teach? When she offers to let you pet a smallish **skein** of soft **merino**, you may think she is doing you a favor but beware—merino is a gateway drug to the harder stuff like **alpaca** and **cashmere**, and don't think she doesn't know it.

Dealers are also most often users. Heck, one of the reasons many of them opened their own stores in the first place was so they could taste the new goods before the general public. When you do decide to succumb to the lure of the yarn, feel free to let your dealer guide your choice. I would venture to say that in no other specialty does the store owner spend as much time with their wares.

DECREASE *noun*: A decrease is a stitch used for shaping, and will give you one or two fewer stitches per row whenever you do one. There are several ways to decrease, and which one you use will depend on how you want the finished item to look—some decreases lean left, and some lean right. The most common decreases are **knit** 2 together (in which you, um, knit two together) and PSSO (short for pass **slipped stitch** over—usually you knit 1, slip 1, then pass the knit stitch over the slipped stitch, although your pattern will tell you exactly what PSSO means to that particular **designer**).

Decreases are only good if you are doing them on purpose. While you may think, "What's one less stitch on the row here and there in the grand scheme of things?" you will undoubtedly find out as soon as you try to stuff a body part into a turtle-neck, sleeve, or sweater body that has decreased too quickly. Calling extra decreases **design modifications** won't work if you can't breathe.

DESIGNER *noun*: The person who thought up (in his or her warped little brain) the sweater you now covet and who made up the model, wrote out a pattern, and now claims that you can get the exact same results. Genius or Spawn of Satan? Your opinion of a particular designer will often rest on how difficult to follow you find his or her patterns. Do they read easily and have math that works out? Does the garment you end up with bear more than a passing resemblance to the photo? Genius. Are there 1,500 pages of **errata**, a **gauge** achievable only in the atmosphere of Venus on alternate Wednesdays, and a pattern that only comes written for a petite small? Spawn of Satan.

To some extent, designers get a bad rap. They don't make typos or math errors on purpose, and sometimes they don't make them at all, but errors are introduced in the editing or printing process. And many, if not most, designers will answer questions if you have them—they want you to make their wonderful designs and be happy while you are doing it. After all, designers were knitters first, and we all know that all knitters are wonderful folks.

DESIGN MODIFICATION *noun*: **Mistake**. As in, "The fact that one sleeve is five inches longer than the other is not a mistake, it is a design modification." Can also be used to excuse **dropped stitches**, off-center **cables**, and color work not found in nature. Much like a cat falling off a table and then glaring at any human who might have seen it as if to say, "I meant to do that," you meant your project to look exactly the way it came out. Should any intrepid soul at your knitting group point out a mistake, all you need to do is to smile enigmatically and say "That isn't a mistake, it is a design modification. I think slavishly following a **designer**'s pattern shows a shocking lack of creativity on the part of the knitter, don't you?" No one will ever say anything negative about your knitting again. Asymmetry is in. And if it isn't when you are reading this, perhaps you could start a new trend.

DEVIL INCARNATE *noun*: See **moth**.

DOLLARS PER HOUR *noun:* A method of rationalizing any outrageously expensive yarn purchase by dividing the sum of money you have spent by the number of hours you could conceivably work on the project and itemizing the result as part of your entertainment budget. It normally goes a little something like "If I went to see a first-run movie at a theater and had a medium soda and a popcorn, I would have been amused (or not) for a total of about two hours at a cost of $18.00, meaning I paid $9.00 per hour for entertainment. If I spend $400.00 on yarn for a sweater that will take me approximately 50 hours to finish, then I am only spending $8.00 an hour for entertainment, as well as having the certainty that the knitting will keep me happy (whereas the movie has some risk), so it is much more efficient as well as fiscally responsible to buy the $400.00 worth of **alpaca** and give up the $18.00 worth of movie." **Sock** knitters are particularly well known for this flavor of rationalization—no one in their right mind would spend $50.00 on a pair of socks, but look at it from a dollars-per-hour standpoint, because socks take a while to **knit**, and even the most extreme sock yarn purchase looks like the bargain of the century.

DOUBLE KNITTING *noun*: If one layer of woolly goodness provides protection from the elements, how much better would two layers be? Double knitting is a technique in which you wind up with a double-thick fabric with wrong sides facing, leaving you with a right side on either side, which makes your project reversible. It is most often worked in two colors to show off an **intarsia** pattern. All the stitches for both sides of the work are held on the same needle, alternating so that you work every other stitch with a different working yarn.

DOUBLE POINTED NEEDLES (DPNs) *noun*: Also known as Devilishly Persnickety Needles. Sold in sets of four or five and available in lengths from five inches to eight inches and in almost any material, DPNs are straight needles that are pointed on both ends. They are used to avoid seaming by **knitting in the round**, so are great for things like **socks** and sleeves. There are those (like me) who learned to **knit** in the round on these things and therefore don't care much for **circular needles**, and those who learned to knit in the round on circulars and therefore may not care much for DPNs. It is all a matter of personal preference, but circulars only get but so small, so when knitting something tiny or knitting a flat circle that either starts or ends with just a few stitches, DPNs are a big help.

They also have a tendency to both multiply and disappear. There are all sorts of clever needle holders on the market to keep your DPNs together, but especially in the smaller sizes that we need to feed our sock addictions, you will never ever have the same number twice. Because they like to hide, you see.

Common DPN hiding places are under the couch cushions, under the passenger seat in the car (because please tell me you aren't knitting socks while driving!), and any dimly lit corner of your **project bag**. You will find them in your lap when you get up, under the chair you like to sit in when you knit, stuck in your hair or behind your eyeglasses, and the more voluptuous amongst us might even discover one in her cleavage. So you scrounge and you fudge and you buy more sets of DPNs.

Eventually the day will come when you can't take it anymore, and you go on a mission to clean up and organize all of your knitting tools and **stash**. Side note: Be sure you schedule several days to do this—those who claim to have accomplished this task in an afternoon are either suffering a severe lack of stash or a severe lack of understanding of the word "organized." Anyway, you clean and you sort and you **frog** and you organize, and what do you find? Hundreds of DPNs, more than you could ever have possibly bought, even during your worst fits of **startitis**.

My theory is that the hiding part of their life cycle is an important part of the DPN mating ritual. Because once they have spent some time out of your sight, they show up in record numbers, and they all look alike! Clearly science hasn't gotten a complete handle on the breeding habits, however, or all of those starving bio majors would be running DPN mills and selling the results of their unholy experiments on eBay. Perhaps some federal funding is necessary to research this maddening conundrum. Write your congressperson and express your opinion that this is how federal monies should be spent—they have certainly funded dumber ideas.

DPNs *noun*: See **double pointed needles**.

DROPPED STITCH *noun*: 1. Damn, you are cruising along on a simple pattern, watching your trash **television** program of choice, and you notice you have one less stitch on the row than you should. Looking back umpteen rows, you realize that one measly little stitch slid off the needle without being worked. And it is merrily unraveling itself like a run in cheap pantyhose before the most important meeting of your life. You need to pick this stitch up before it gets any farther away from where it should be, and you might also need to **frog** a few rows to do it. Damn. 2. Yeah! The clever **designer** wanted a laddered effect and has written the pattern so you can drop some stitches! On purpose! There is something so freeing about making what amounts to a **mistake** on purpose. Dropping stitches makes me feel like a knitting renegade, thumbing my nose at the anti-dropped-stitch establishment. OK, maybe that's just me. But dropped stitches can be fun. Yeah!

DUPLICATE STITCH *noun*: **Intarsia** got you down, yet you can't live without a little bit of two-color detail in your sweater? Duplicate stitch is a form of embroidery in which a contrasting color of yarn is threaded through a **tapestry needle** and

41

worked over an existing stitch or series of stitches to make a pattern. So you can **knit** mindlessly away on your stockinette sweater while you are engrossed in the M*A*S*H marathon on cable **television**, and go back and embroider in your stitched sheep or monogram or what-have- you when your attention is completely focused on what you are doing (and not on "Hot Lips" Houlihan). It makes the knitting easier, although it may make the **finishing** process longer.

DYE LOT *noun*: Huzzah, you have found the pattern of your dreams and chosen the perfect yarn. Huzzah again, you need 27 **skeins** and there happen to be 28 left in the store. You gather them up and look for the dye lot numbers. There are three different ones. This is bad. Put the yarn back in the bin and step away from it. It is perfect no more.

While knitters make **design modifications**, dyers . . . well, I don't exactly know what the hell it is that dyers do differently, but the dye lot number is on the yarn **label** to show you what skeins of yarn came through the same dye bath at about the same time. Dying is an art as well as a science, and sometimes Tuesday's dye bath doesn't look exactly like Monday's did. They both look good, mind you, they just aren't the same. What happens when you use two different dye lots in your project? Sometimes nothing. Most of the time you get a stripe at the row where you changed skeins. Sometimes it is a very faint variation, and you can blame the eyesight of the person who is rude enough to point it out to you. Sometimes it is a huge difference, and you can go with design modification. Most often though, the difference is just enough to piss you off—not close enough to get away with and too close to look like a two-color design. You know it is there, and there isn't squat you can do about it if you didn't notice in time.

If you should happen to get home with two dye lots of something and you are partway through a sweater and reading this entry made you break out into a cold sweat, there are a few tricks to try. First, call the store where you bought the yarn and see if they have any skeins left of the dye lot you already started to work with. You may be able to do an exchange. Next, compare the dye lots and see if they might be close enough to get away with. In that case, try to make sure you don't have multiple dye lots in one garment piece—do the front in dye lot one and the back in dye lot two and hope no one stares at your shoulder **seams**. If you must use two dye lots in one piece, avoid the stripe issue when changing skeins by doing one last full row of dye lot one, the next row doing every other stitch in dye lot one and dye lot two, and the following rows in dye lot two.

When all else fails, it is off to the **frog pond**. The good news is, you then have a perfect excuse to go back to the yarn store and buy more yarn.

EASE *noun*: 1. Simply put, ease is the amount of difference between what your body part measurement actually is and the amount of fabric needed to cover said body part comfortably and without producing an X rating in the movie that is your life. For example, if you have a 36-inch bust and you measure your favorite sweater, you might notice that the bust measurement of the finished garment is actually not 36 inches. Typically it will be between 38 inches and 40 inches. This gives you room to do things like move, eat, or breathe.

Different **designers** handle ease differently, which is why it is important to check the finished garment measurements shown at the top of a pattern and not just **knit** up a size medium because that's what you always make. 2. Another great word to throw at someone who has the temerity to comment on the fit of your hand-knit garment. Her: "Did you lose 50 pounds since you finished that sweater?" You: "No, it's ease." See also **design modification**.

EASE, NEGATIVE *noun*: Now that I just told you that **ease** makes things bigger, I should probably point out that bigger is not always better. For garments that need a tight fit, be it a pair of **socks** or a sweater or skirt that you will wear to emphasize your, um, assets, you need to make sure the finished garment measurement is less than the actual body part measurement. A sock without negative ease will fall down—the **ribbing** at the top needs something to grab onto in its fight against gravity. Negative ease is most important when working with stretchy stitch patterns like ribbing.

ENGLISH KNITTING *noun*: English style knitters (and you don't have to be from England to be one) hold their working yarn in their right hands and "throw" it to create their stitches. English knitting is thought to be slower than **Continental knitting**, but whatever method you use can be pretty darn quick if you spend enough time doing it. Not that I have a chip on my shoulder about this speed thing, being an English knitter, not me.

ENTRELAC *noun:* An incredibly clever way to **knit short row** triangles and squares so that you wind up with a textural checkerboard. Entrelac has its staunch supporters and its rabid haters. Die-hard entrelackers (entrelacians? entrelacticians?) have been known to learn how to **purl** backward so they don't have to do all that pesky turning of the rows. Which goes to show that entrelac knitting has a few addictive qualities, much like knitting in general. My theory is that the knitters who love entrelac somehow feel that they are thumbing their collective noses at the **finishing** fairies. "Look," they can say, "I have knitted a fabric of twelve billion tiny squares, yet I didn't have to sew them together! Hah!" At least, that's my theory.

ERRATA *noun:* Patterns can contain **mistakes**. **Designers** make mistakes when they are trying to write one pattern in 1,500 sizes. Editors make mistakes when they have read their fifteenth pattern of the day, and the K2togs all blur together. Typesetters and other folks in book production can make mistakes because they are *gasp* not knitters. Bad stuff happens to good patterns.

Eagle-eyed knitters make the pattern and figure out that there are mistakes. Someone tells the designer. The designer figures out what the problem is and writes a correction. The corrections are called errata. (Of course there are errata for non-knitting books as well, but who really cares?) A quick Internet search on "name of pattern book errata" will tell you pretty quickly if any exist. And usually pattern corrections are incorporated into later printings of a book.

EYELASH *noun*: 1. That which those in the know about your magic knitting powers will bat at you in order to get you to **knit** them the garment of their dreams (or their eight hundredth pair of hand-knitted **socks**—boy, are those addictive!) 2. A type of yarn that has itty-bitty, skinny, usually synthetic fibers hanging off of it that flutter in the breeze after the item is knitted. Eyelash is considered a **novelty yarn**. I believe the novelty wears off pretty quickly.

FAIR ISLE *noun*: 1. A smallish island located
halfway between Orkney and Shetland in the
Atlantic Ocean, home to many sheep and not so
many people. 2. A type of knitting that scares me
to death. Fair Isle knitting is color work **knit** in
the round, in which the colored yarns are carried
across the back of the work when not in use, and
steeks are used to create openings for the arms,
neckline, or center front opening. In traditional
Fair Isle no more than two colors are used in any
one row, although there can be several colors

employed in the entire project. You have to be a pretty serious knitter to attempt a Fair Isle sweater, but the results are magnificent.

FELT *noun*: Fabric that is created by fibers adhering to each other rather than by being woven. The good stuff is thick and luscious and made of animal fibers. This is not to be confused with the bad stuff, which is made of **acrylic** and is the basis for many a school or craft project gone wrong.

FELT *verb*: The process of turning animal fibers into felt fabric. 1. A very bad thing that happens when someone in your household (never the knitter of course) puts a sweater that took three years to **knit** out of very expensive **wool** in the washer and dryer. It becomes the most expensive piece of clothing your three-year-old will ever own, exhibit 37-A in your pending divorce trial, or if you are very crafty and can sew, a handbag with which to beat the perpetrator. 2. A very good thing that happens when you do it on purpose. Knit an extra-large garment or bag in a yarn that is at least 70 percent wool or other animal fiber, agitate it in hot water with a bit of soap and a pair of jeans, and with careful supervision you get controlled shrinkage that makes a thick, soft, very comfortable wool fabric. Much like knitting, felting is highly addictive, and you will find yourself felting everything that doesn't run away first. And once you get handy at it, you can felt one of your soon-to-be-ex-husband's favorite sweaters down for your three-year-old and see how *he* likes it.

FINISHED OBJECT (FO) *noun*: The holy grail of knitting. Difficult to attain, not because of the knitting part but because of the finished part. Finished means completely finished—ends woven in, **seams** sewn up, buttons sewn on. Some folks even put a cute little label in the back. No cheating by calling the loose ends **fringe** and the lack of buttons a **design modification**. For an object to be truly finished, it needs to require no further work.

FINISHING *verb*: This little word is a lot trickier than it looks. If you have knitted all of the pieces of your project and now all you need to do is whip them up into the **finished object**, the things you have left to do are loosely grouped together and called finishing. There are those folks out there who enjoy finishing, but for most knitters I know, it is the actual knitting (or occasionally shopping for yarn and casting on projects) that is the fun part, and the **blocking**, seaming, button-sewing-on, collar-picking-up, toe **grafting**, weaving-in-two-million-ends sorts of things are tasks to be dreaded. Because to tell the truth, there are projects in which the finishing takes longer than the knitting did.

There are two good ways I know to solve this problem. The first is to take a finishing project to your local **sit-and-knit night**. Sometimes good company can make a distasteful task go more quickly, and if you are a complete klutz, someone might take pity on you and maybe sew on a button or two because they can't stand to see you screw it up anymore. The other is to offer cold hard cash (or warm woolly yarn) to someone at the **LYS** or to one of those twisted folks who think finishing is cool and have them do the finishing for you. On the one hand, having someone else do your finishing feels a little bit like cheating. But on the other, the item is still completely hand made (although not by your hands), and you are bringing great joy (or cold, hard cash or warm, woolly goodness) to someone else who doesn't hate finishing as much as you do.

Whatever method you choose to keep yourself on the finishing straight and narrow, remember this—no matter how much you dread doing it, it is absolutely imperative that your project is finished before it has time to go completely out of style. You may rescue the occasional trendy project if you live long enough that your adult daughter could wear it when it comes back in (if you are single and childless now, so much the better—you have more time), but there is no worse feeling than finally girding your loins and wading into the finishing fray only to discover that there is no stinking way you are going to be caught dead in public in the garment you just finished.

FO *noun*: See **finished object**.

FRINGE *noun*: Strands of yarn that are knotted onto the end of a project, often a scarf, for decorative effect. It is cheating to refuse to weave in your ends and call them fringe, which isn't to say that you can't try it.

FROG *verb*: Ripping out worked rows to get to the row before you made the **mistake**. Not for the faint of heart (it is frightening to see all those live stitches floating in the breeze without the anchor of the **knitting needle**), but it is very often the quickest solution to a knitting problem. The word comes from the sound the frog makes—ribbit ribbit = rip-it rip-it.

Some people are fearless in the practice of frogging, and some avoid it like the plague. Those who have enough self-knowledge to understand that they will go slowly insane in a *Gaslight* sort of way knowing there is a mistake in their work, even though the mistake they made is tiny and probably invisible to the naked eye of a non-knitter, will soon be expert froggers. Those who refer to mistakes as **design modifications** will probably never frog a row in their lives. See also **lifeline** and **tink**.

FROG POND *noun*: The place where unloved **UFOs** and **WIPs** go to await their froggy fate. Far from the lovely visual image the term connotes, most frog ponds are located in the bottoms of closets, in ugly straw souvenir tote bags from trips your parents made you go on, or under sofas and armchairs. The bad news about having a frog pond is that those projects tend to represent a lot of wasted hours. The good news is that frogging is a great way to take out your aggression without harming anything living—just hook up your loose end to a **ball winder** or **swift** and shred, baby, shred. Instant destruction, tantrum averted, and now you get to think about what you want to make out of all the lovely yarn you just liberated.

FUN FUR *noun*: A total misnomer, fun fur is never real fur and is rarely much fun to **knit**. On the one hand, it tends to be a little stiff to work with, which can be frustrating for a new knitter. On the other hand, even if you were to drop 1,500 stitches, you pretty much can't see any **mistakes** through the **acrylic** haze. I know there are folks out there who like fun fur; I am just not one of them. So please, use it responsibly.

GARTER STITCH *noun*: On straight needles, **knit** every row. When working in the round, knit one row, **purl** one row. Yawn . . . oh, sorry, was I talking about garter stitch? I nodded off. While garter stitch in a plain vanilla yarn can induce comalike boredom, it is a great choice for working with a fussy or glitzy novelty yarn that would overpower a more complicated stitch pattern. Another benefit to garter stitch is that it doesn't roll in on itself like a scroll the way that **stockinette** stitch does, making it the perfect border for scarves, garment pieces, and even the heel flaps of **socks**.

GAUGE *noun*: Also called **tension**, especially in European patterns. Gauge is the number of stitches and rows per inch that you are more than likely to get when you use the suggested (either on the ball band of the yarn or in a pattern) combination of needles and yarn. I am about to tell you something that most knitters don't want to hear: If you are going to make a garment that has to fit a specific person, you have to get gauge. You really, really do. Really.

No one wants to do a gauge **swatch** because it is boring, and it is much more fun to just **cast on** and leap blindly into a new sweater. While this process may work for you if you have a wide variety of friends in a wide variety of sizes and will just give the finished project to whomever it looks like it might fit, it is a little slapdash if you want to make something for someone specific. A few minutes, or even hours, spent on a gauge swatch will prevent days of heartbreak in your future.

Make sure your swatch is a minimum of four inches square—a smaller square might skew your measurements because stitches tend to be tighter near edges. Use the pattern stitch you are planning on using, the yarn you have chosen, and the exact needles you will be using. If you are working your garment in the round, make sure you **knit** your swatch in the round. Many of us have different gauge in the round than we do knitting back and forth in rows. Now measure your work in the center of the square to avoid those pesky edges and compare your number to the numbers in the pattern.

If your numbers are exact, say amen and go to town; you are ready to cast on. If you get fewer stitches and rows per inch than the pattern requires, go down a needle size or two and try again. If you get more stitches and rows per inch than the pattern requires, go up a needle size or two and try again. You will eventually get gauge.

Are there times when gauge doesn't matter? Yes and no. If your gauge is off when you are knitting a scarf it might not be a big deal. Scarves aren't exactly demanding so far as fit goes. But if your gauge is way off in one direction or the other, you might get a fabric you don't care for or run out of yarn way before you had planned to stop. We still tease my sister about the "lead blanket" she made for her first grandchild. The gauge was so tight she used up a metric ton of yarn, and the fabric was so dense it almost didn't bend. Had she gone up a needle size or ten, her end result would have been much more pleasing, although the blanket might not then have been as much use as it was for preventing the baby from rolling off the couch (or moving, but that's another issue).

What if you positively can't get the specified gauge for the project you want to make? Try a different yarn or different needles, and if you still can't get close, you might want to try a different project altogether, at least for now.

GENIUS *noun*: See **designer**.

GRAFTING *verb*: The process by which two sets of live stitches are invisibly sewn together. Grafting is commonly used for the toes of **socks** and on shawl and scarf patterns that need each half to be worked separately to keep the pattern on the ends facing in the right direction. Grafting also tends to lead to **throwing** (the second definition), cursing, crying, and expressing a preference to stick size 0000 **DPNs** in your eyeballs.

If the idea of grafting makes you shudder in terror, the conservative knitter would advocate practicing to become perfect. Me? I would see if I could use a three-needle **bind off** and call whatever **seam** results a **design modification**. See also **Kitchener stitch**.

GUSSET *noun*: 1. A wedge or triangle-shaped piece that is used in the construction of closely fitted garments, most often seen in **socks** or the underarms of thick sweaters. 2. What your scarf will soon look like if you get carried away with unintended **decreases**.

HANDSPUN *adjective*: Yarn made by one person using a drop spindle or a spinning wheel. Handspun yarn can run the gamut from fingering **weight** to chunky and can be available in small **skeins** or tons of yardage. Handspun yarn can be more expensive than commercially made yarn, but that makes perfect sense because it takes a good amount of time to make.

After you have been knitting for a while, the urge to learn to spin so you can make your own handspun yarn begins to creep up on you. Beware! **Spinning** is a hobby that is almost as addictive as knitting! Soon you will have a **roving stash** to equal your yarn stash, and you won't be able to walk completely around your bed because the wheel and the drop spindles are in the way. Next you will want to buy livestock, so you can raise your own fiber; then you will have to move to a rural area, with or without your family. Maybe you should just stick to buying handspun yarn from others for the time being.

HANK *noun*: A unit of yarn for sale that is essentially a giant loop rather than a wound **skein**. Hanks need to be made into balls before they are used, or you will spend all of your free time untangling rather than knitting. You can use a chair back or a willing (or unwilling) pair of hands to hold the loop open while you wind, or you can invest in a **swift** and a **ball winder**. Actually, frequently using a pair of unwilling hands to wind skeins is a really quick way to ensure you will receive a beautiful swift and ball winder for the next gift-giving occasion, which is a fine thing. Profess a desire to wind off enough hanks, and your friends and family members will be searching under the couch cushions for spare change and running to the **LYS** as soon as possible. "Happy Wednesday, Mom, here's a gift!"

I-CORD *noun*: A clever cord made by knitting a small number of stitches on a **DPN** over and over (and over and over and over) without turning the work. It sounds sort of odd, but once you get the hang of it, it becomes an instant gratification sort of thing that you will want to add to many of your projects. I-cord is used as thick **fringe**, to finish the tops of hats **knit** in the round, and as an applied finish to garments. The only thing I have not been able to combine with my I-cord fetish is my sock-making fetish—there doesn't seem to be any real need for I-cord on **socks**.

INCREASE *noun*: A stitch used for shaping that gives you one or two more stitches per row whenever you do one. This is a fine idea if you are doing it on purpose. Be aware that many beginning knitters wind up with increases all over the place because they are either splitting yarn and knitting the individual **plies** separately, making **yarn overs** where none need to be, or because they aren't completing the stitch properly by pushing the worked stitch off of the left needle. Unchecked increases are a quick way to get an extra-large sweater when you **cast on** for a small.

INTARSIA *noun*: Knitting with two or more colors, in which each color section is worked with its own ball of yarn. Intarsia knitting is essentially knitting in a picture—a smiley face, a scattering of flowers, *The Last Supper*. If you **knit** the color changes in rather than embroidering them on later, you are doing intarsia. The important part of working in intarsia is to make sure you are twisting the working yarns consistently when switching from one color to the next. Otherwise you will wind up with holes between the different colored sections, or your smiley face will drop out of the knitting completely.

JOIN, FELTED *noun:* A technique for adding one ball of animal fiber yarn to the next by felting the two ends together, which helps avoid having a million ends to weave in during the **finishing** stage. Actually, I think some very ladylike knitter made up this term because she didn't want to say **spit splice** in public. See also **join, Russian**.

JOIN, RUSSIAN *noun:* Like a **spit splice**, a Russian join is a way to **felt** the end of one ball of yarn to the beginning of the next. A spit splice works best when joining two balls of the same yarn, while a Russian join works best for attaching two different yarns, for example, when you are doing **intarsia**. Fray about two to three inches of each yarn end, then cross the two yarn ends over each other about three to four inches from the end. Now fold each end back onto itself. You have a looped join in the middle, and the frayed ends are on top of the same color of yarn. Now follow the instructions for the spit splice and voila—a two-color **felted join**. What any of this has to do with Russia is not immediately apparent to me.

KAL *noun*: See **knit along**.

KIP *verb*: See **knitting in public**.

KITCHENER STITCH *noun*: Who is this Kitchener guy anyway, and can I please smack him in the head? I *hate* to **graft** the toes of **socks**, and I pretty much love everything else there is to love about the sock-making process. While it doesn't seem like anything can be proven, urban knitting legend has it that the Kitchener stitch is named after Lord Herbert Horatio Kitchener, former governor of Sudan and an active member of the British military until his death in 1916 (so I can't smack him in the head, he is already way dead). Kitchener is alleged to have requested that the women at home during World War I **knit** socks to his specifications, which included a seamless toe for the soldiers' comfort. His name stuck to the grafted toe used for the seamless sock—thus the Kitchener stitch. I have to say that I wonder if Lord Kitchener is spinning in his grave because his name is better known as a knitting stitch to be sworn over than for his military achievements. I don't think for a minute that as he was busy fighting the Boer War that he thought, "Well, this is all very exciting, but I would really prefer to be remembered into eternity for my contributions to the art of sock knitting."

KNIT ALONG (KAL) *noun*: Sort of a group case of **startitis** (maybe it *is* contagious!) in which a whole group of knitters, whether online or in real life, decide to make the same project at the same time and compare strategies and results while they work. This can be a great way to foster camaraderie and creativity, or an insanely competitve race to the finish line, depending on the knitters involved. I admit to being a serial KAL dropout—I really think I am gong to see it through when I sign on, but somehow I never quite get the right project done in the right order. But aside from fellowship (or competition), the coolest thing about KALs is being able to see all of the variety that can occur due to the interpretation of one pattern by many individual knitters. It seems like no two projects are exactly the same, and I mean that in a good way.

KNITTING IN PUBLIC (KIP) *verb*: The first time I saw this acronym I was really surprised. In my younger days, acronyms were things to beware of. (Remember going to detention for PDA—Public Displays of Affection? Me either. I was a total geek in high school, but I *knew of* people who got busted for that.) So why should there be an acronym for something as harmless as knitting? (Well, harmless unless you have an addictive personality, but I digress. Again.) Rightly or wrongly, there are knitters and non-knitters alike who think that knitting in public is a little strange.

One reason not to KIP is a fear of speaking to strangers. You whip a knitting project out of your briefcase on a bus, and someone is bound to start talking to you. Maybe they want to know what you are making; maybe they want you to know that their grandmother or some other family member **knits**. Maybe they want to tell you they know how to knit, or that they could never knit because they don't have the time, or that the color you are working in reminds them of their childhood doll, or whatever. Knitting in public leads to chatting with strangers; it just does. If you don't like chatting with strangers, you may want to limit your KIPing.

I don't mind chatting with strangers, so I pretty much KIP all the time. I am a high-energy person (read: fidgety and impatient) and KIPing makes my life and the lives of those around me much happier in instances where if I put my needles down I may have to strangle someone, preferably someone who is in line in front of me.

Sometimes, KIPers are knitting missionaries in disguise. Admire their speedy stitches and the next thing you know they have whipped out some spare needles and yarn from their capacious **project bags** and are giving impromptu classes on the subway. And they are having such a great time that you almost wonder if they had somewhere to go in the first place, or if they were just hanging out on the express train looking for people to convert.

KIPing can also inspire fear in others, which, if you are just a little power hungry, can be a lot of fun. If you are a lot power hungry than you probably need something a little more aggressive than a set of five **DPNs** to get the reaction you want. I frightened the living heck out of a Finnair flight attendant last year while working on a sock, which surprised me since I had successfully gotten the DPNs past security in three countries. Some folks just don't know what knitting looks like.

Which leads me to some folks just don't know what knitting looks like in a good way. Sometimes when I am knitting away at my daughter's dance class, kids who clearly come from families with no knitters come and sit by me to see what I am working on. Just the other day, a seven-year-old boy saw me coming in from the cold and said, "Oh, I see you finished your blue scarf. It looks very nice on you," making the connection in his nonknitter mind between a ball of yarn and a fashion statement. I may not be converting them into knitters, but I am planting subconscious seeds for the knitting missionaries to harvest in years to come.

KNIT *verb*: An activity that brings us closer to nirvana by providing an outlet for our creativity, hostility, and any spare cash we might have lying around . . . sometimes all at the same time.

KNIT *noun*: There are really only two stitches in knitting: knit and **purl**. That's it. Everything else is a combination of or a variation on these two stitches. If you happen to like doing **garter stitch** on straight needles or **stockinette** in the round, you can pretty much go months at a time without even having to purl. The knit stitch is the one where your **working yarn** is held in back of the needles.

KNITTING IN THE ROUND *verb*: Knitting in the round is just what it sounds like—instead of knitting back and forth in rows on straight needles, you **knit** round and round and round on a **circular needle,** or a multiple of **DPNs**.

Seven reasons why knitting in the round is the coolest thing ever:

1. You can get away with making **at the end of the row** take up to a week, as long as you are subtle about moving the **stitch marker**.
2. You can make anything out of a tube—a sock, a hat, a purse, a sleeping bag—and you can try things on as you go.
3. You never have to **purl** if you don't want to.
4. With a little forethought, you can avoid having to sew any **seams** at all, ever.
5. You will never be unarmed. As noted elsewhere, **circular needles** make excellent garrotes, and DPNs can be very threatening when waved about in a menacing manner.
6. **Steeks**, if you are inclined toward the dramatic gesture of cutting up knitting, or have a desire to make your less self-assured knitter friends faint dead away.
7. The only way to truly screw things up is if you twist the first row when joining, and if you do that, you can always keep knitting and call your project a **Moebius**.

KNOT *noun*: 1. What you should never, ever make when changing from one **skein** of yarn to the next. 2. What you do not want to see in your yarn, but often do, in the middle of a row, especially in a **lace** pattern.

Basically, there should be no knots in knitting. If you need to change skeins, do it at the end of a row, and if one of the **felted joins** won't work for you, leave a tail hanging so you can weave in the ends later. If you find a knot in your working yarn, cut it out and treat the two ends as you normally would when changing skeins. If you find a lot of knots in one skein of yarn, bring it to the attention of the **LYS** where you bought it or the manufacturer. No one sends out skeins like that on purpose, and you may be able to get it replaced.

LABEL *noun:* Every **skein** of yarn you purchase should have a label on it. Common bits of information found on the label are: the manufacturer (the company or person to curse when you find your first knot), the color name or number (which will never be "green" but "Misty Morning Moss in Maine"), the **dye lot** number (589863745142XX 93874869762YYYYZ), fiber content (.2 percent expensive luxury fiber, 99.8 percent things you never heard of), **weight** designation of the yarn (dental floss to rope), weight of the skein in grams or ounces (anyone notice the drug parallel again here? "Yo, dude, I scored 350 grams of prime Mongolian **cashmere** this weekend, it was aaaaaaaaaaaweseome"), yardage in yards or meters (although to be fair it should really just say, "Ten less yards than you need, so go buy another one"), and sometimes care instructions (which never seem to include, "leave it to the side of your laundry pile and eventually it will air out because you are too scared to wash a hand knit").

Even if you wind your **hanks** into balls as soon as you acquire your yarn, it is a good idea to have a system for keeping labels near the yarn they came from. Guaranteed, the day you chuck all the labels is the day you forget some pertinent piece of information about the skein you are looking at, and you make a bad decision.

LACE *noun*: Knitted lace is a wondrous thing. Usually worked from a charted pattern, chock full of **increases**, **decreases**, and **yarn overs** to give an open effect, often done on small needles with very fine yarn, lace will take hours and hours of work and then come off of your needles looking like a nasty clump of limp spaghetti. You will avert your face in disgust. But after a little **blocking**, your lace work will look so amazing you won't be able to believe you did it yourself. Non-knitters will swoon at your feet because no mere mortal should be able to produce such fine work. Really, lace is very impressive.

I have to admit that after years of resistance, I have started a lace shawl. It requires my full and total attention, which I don't always have to give. When it gets near the end, it will have something like two kazillion and twelve stitches in each row, meaning each row will take me about a week (and lends new meaning to the **at the end of the row** method of telling time.) I may finish it by the time I am ninety, but I may not. But when it is done, I will know that I spent some time working on a thing of beauty that will last forever (or until my daughter inherits it and uses it for a dog to lie on, but I try not to think about those things).

A bit of handy information about lace knitting is that it is a thrifty way to get more knitting hours for your yarn buck. Even a relatively expensive **skein** of lace-weight yarn will have thousands of yards on it, and it will take a good long time to **knit** it all up—giving you a very favorable return on your investment from a dollars per hour value perspective.

LIFELINE *noun*: A very handy technique perfected by **lace** knitters to mark a row that was correctly executed. Choose a very fine yarn that contrasts with your project, and run the yarn through every stitch on a row you are sure is correct. Then keep knitting. As you progress through the rows, on occasion you may want to move your lifeline closer to the row you are knitting. If the unthinkable occurs and you have more, um, anomalies in a row than you can live with, you can **frog** just the few iffy rows, knowing that the lifeline will prevent you from dropping stitches back for a hundred or so rows. The difference between your knitting project and the Titanic is this: For the ocean liner, lifelines were thrown after the ship was going down. In lace knitting, you have to remember to place the lifeline when things are cruising right along. If you wait until you hit the iceberg, it will be too late. Maybe there aren't so many differences after all.

LOCAL YARN STORE (LYS) *noun*: Mecca for knitters; the place that cures all of your ills, just by spending time within the comfort of its four walls. Home to every little thing that you need to **knit** with and people who will understand your knitting lifestyle and will never judge the amount of disposable income your **stash** represents. Yes, you can buy yarn and supplies online, and there are even Internet chat rooms where knitters keep each other company, but none of these can replace the joy of the LYS. You should support the LYS whenever possible, lest it close its doors forever. When your significant other questions your spending, you can safely point out that you are not overspending on yarn you don't yet need; you are using your dollars to enrich your life and the lives of others by ensuring that the knitting life as we know it will always live on. Anthemic background music may support your point, as long as you are pretty subtle about turning it on.

LYS *noun*: See **local yarn store**.

MAGIC LOOP *noun*: A lot of folks prefer **knitting in the round** on **circular needles** rather than **DPNs**, but circular needles only get so short, and even if you found one that was shorter than usual, it would be difficult to make a small diameter circle. So, many patterns call for a circular needle for the body of the work and then suggest changing to DPNs for the narrower parts. The magic loop technique is an adventure in extreme DPN avoidance. Half the stitches are on one end of the needle, and the other half rest on the cable between the ends. At the end of each half of the round, you pull the cable through and switch the stitches' orientation. There are many things about knitting that I consider to be magic, and I have to say this technique was never one of them. But there is something to be said for being able to truthfully say you are working magic when a non-knitter asks you what you are doing.

MARKER, STITCH *noun*: Stitch markers are sort of like potato chips: Once you have one and realize how good it is, you will want more and more and more. The most common stitch markers are thin rings that hang on the needle between two stitches to designate the beginning of a round or the start of a repeat. Plastic ring markers are available in several sizes and colors and are very inexpensive. But many artisans make gorgeous rings out of metal wire that are decorated with all sorts of charms, beads, or other little bitty decorative items. Available online, at **LYSs**, and at **sheep and wool festivals**, you will find yourself snatching them up whenever you see an appealing one. Go for it—we should all support local artisans and it is much easier to hide one hundred stitch markers than it is to hide one hundred skeins of yarn.

If you need to mark a specific stitch as opposed to a specific spot in a row or round, you will need a split ring stitch marker that will lock onto the stitch itself. In that case, the lightweight plastic ones are the best because they don't weigh enough to pull the stitch out of shape.

MERINO WOOL *noun*: Wool that comes from merino sheep, a breed known for its fine, soft fleece. When our mothers and aunties complain about the scratchy wool that they had to **knit** with in decades past, they are usually fondling some merino and are in shock at the time. Back in the dawn of time, you bought wool or not-wool, whereas today, not only can you buy wool with the breed designation on it, you can probably buy wool with the name of the sheep it came from on there, too. ("Hey, look, I am knitting with 100 percent Shirley the sheep!") There are many other sheep breeds whose wool is soft and lovely, but merino is one of the most common.

MISTAKE *noun*: For pattern errors such as mis-crossed **cables** or uneven blocks in basket weave, you need to consider whether you wish to **tink**, **frog**, or just banish the **WIP** to the back of the closet where it will fade into a distant, vaguely unpleasant memory. For variations such as a square neckline when you meant to make a scoop or one sleeve longer than the other, rejoice! You haven't made a mistake, you have made a design modification. See also **design modification**.

MOEBIUS *noun*: A scarf based on a mathematical principle, a Moebius ring or Moebius loop is a circular piece of knitting with one permanent twist in the fabric. I firmly believe that this style came about because some knitter got sloppy with joining the first row when **knitting in the round**, but I have no proof. If I am right, this is a genius example of someone turning a **mistake** into a **design modification** and not only getting away with it but giving it a name and getting others to make the same mistake on purpose!

MOHAIR *noun*: Mohair yarn comes from **Angora** goats. The younger the goat, the finer the fibers that come from it, which is why you see designations like kid mohair or baby mohair. Mohair has a nice sheen to it, and mohair yarns often have a fluffy or furry appearance, which makes them a total pain to **frog**. The good news is, many tiny

mistakes can be hidden in its lovely fuzziness, so frogging may not be necessary.

MOTH *noun*: The **devil incarnate**, eater of both **stash** and **finished objects**. Should be treated with a zero tolerance attitude. Loving one's fellow creatures is all well and good, until they get near my yarn. You eat my yarn, you are going to have a very short life span indeed, sucker!

MULTIS *noun*: Short for multicolored, a multi yarn has more than one color on the strand. Multis can be self-striping or just provide a random color mix. Knitting with multis is not for the control freak knitter—you don't have a whole lot of control over which color shows up where. If you are the type of knitter who will sit with a ruler and a scale and do surgery to force a color pattern to be symmetrical, you may want to back away from the multis and take up **Fair Isle**. Or valium. See also **pooling**, **self-striping**.

NEEDLE, CABLE *noun*: A spare needle used to hold working **cable** stitches out of the way when needed. The cable needles do not have to be the same size as the knitting needles you are using, which is why they usually only come in two thicknesses. One style looks like a **DPN** with a slight bump in the middle; another looks like a small candy cane. Invariably you will come to the cable row when there is no cable needle to be found (I suspect cable needles cavort with missing DPNs, but I have no scientific proof of this), so feel free to use a regular DPN of any size to get the job done. Of course, you may not be able to find one of those either—creative usage of pens or pencils, unbent paperclips, drinking straws, coffee stirrers, or anything else skinny and short is often called for. The braver knitters amongst use can cable without a needle, but that is maybe not such a hot idea if you are knitting cables for the first time.

NEEDLES, CIRCULAR *noun*: Round and round and round and round she goes and where she stops, nobody knows. Well, you do if you use a **stitch marker**, but I digress. A circular needle has a point on each end (they can be metal, plastic, or **bamboo**, like any other **knitting needle**), and a flexible cable in the middle, and is used when knitting in the round. Because there are all sorts of different sized tubelike parts in knitting (like a **sock**, a hat, or a sleeve), there are different lengths of circular needles; you should choose the length closest to the finished size of your project. They also can be used when knitting back and forth in rows, which is especially useful on projects with a huge number of stitches in each row (the stitches are less likely to fall off the needle when you aren't looking) or something that will weigh quite a bit (the weight of the project is on the cable on your lap, rather than hanging on one straight needle which could tax your wrist). Circular needles are also the things that put the magic in **magic loop** and will make a perfect garrote for the unthinking clod who refused to honor the **at the end of the row** announcement one too many times. See also **knitting in the round**.

NEEDLES, KNITTING *noun*: Those pointy things you **knit** with. They can be wood, plastic, metal, or more exotic materials. They can be straight, **double-pointed**, or **circular**. If you are desperate in an urban setting, they can be two sharpened pencils; if stranded on a desert island, they could be two similarly sized sticks. But knitting doesn't happen without needles.

Yes, I have seen "knitting looms," and yes, I know some folks consider those knitting. I am a purist; I do not.

NEEDLES, TAPESTRY *noun*: Tapestry needles look like hand-sewing needles on steroids. They are thick, have large eyes to thread yarn through, and have a blunt tip so that you neither split the yarn as you are weaving in ends, nor clumsily drive the needle point so far into the tip of your finger that you scream obscenities (again) and bleed all over your **WIP**.

NOVELTY YARNS *noun*: The exact opposite of classic, everyday utility yarns, novelty yarns are often fun and whimsical. They include **fun furs**, **eyelash** yarn, and anything else that when worked up closely resembles the discarded pelt of a stuffed animal. Novelty yarns are often impulse buys, and like long, drawn out **SEX**, these types of purchases seem like a really good idea at the time. Just remember, the primary downfall of novelty yarns is that they are trend driven, and the novelty can wear off pretty quickly as you struggle to **knit** with these furry, fuzzy, glittery, and generally inelastic forms of knitter torture.

The upside of novelty yarns is that they can often be found cheaply, sitting in the bargain bin at the **LYS** once their 15 minutes of fame are over. Items made from novelty yarns have been known to cause inordinate amounts of joy in young girly girls who want their entire world to be sparkly pink and purple. And their half-life is probably roughly equal to that of nuclear waste. After the end of the world as we know it, the cockroaches will have plenty of fun fur scarves to knit.

PHOTOGRAPHY, MODEL *noun*: While many knitters think that **designers** are the **spawn of Satan**, in many cases it is actually the photographer whose neck I would cheerfully wring. In search of the perfect photograph, the photographer experiments with lighting, pose, and focus so that, guaranteed, the one piece of pattern detail you need to see to help you **knit** a garment is the one detail that is cropped out or artfully soft-focused into oblivion. Bonus points if he makes sure that there is never a full-on photo of the model wearing a garment in a setting approximating real life. God forbid you should be able to get an idea how something actually hangs from a pattern book photograph.

PICKING *adjective*: A common term for **Continental knitting**, because the Continental knitter picks the **working yarn** with the tip of her needle rather than **throwing** the working yarn around the needle. Not to be confused with picky, which is what anyone else is who notices a **design modification** in your **FO**.

PICKING UP *verb*: 1. What you do to every single **skein** in a new-to-you **LYS**. Occasionally, but not always, followed by the act of putting down. Well, now that I think of it, you always put it down eventually, it's just that sometimes you put it down in its bin of origin, and sometimes you put it down on the counter so you can have the unfettered joy of watching your credit card melt later in the day. 2. The act of creating a row of live stitches on the edge of a previously **knit** piece. Pssst, don't tell anyone I told you, but that whole process works much more easily if you have a **crochet** hook or two lying around.

PILLING *noun*: Pilling occurs with wear. Little bitty balls of fiber are raised on the surface of the knitted item, where they stick and look ugly. You can get rid of pilling with the judicious use of a sweater shaver or a sweater stone. But be aware that if you wind up shaving one area over and over again, you are probably weakening the fiber overall by removing so much of it. It is hard to turn any serious amount of pilling into a **design modification** because it tends to occur in the small sections that get the most wear. Unless you really can convince an innocent bystander that you wanted furry yarn only at your elbows, cuffs, underarms, and the spot where your favorite purse rubs.

PLY *noun*: If you take the end of a piece of yarn and untwist it a bit until it separates into the individual strands that make it up, each one of these strands is a ply. A yarn can be made up of any number of plies, and the number of plies isn't a reliable indication of the yarn's **weight**, so while one may assume that 12-ply is always thicker than 4-ply, if the 12-ply is made of spider webs and the 4-ply is made of inch-thick **roving**, one would be wrong by a mile.

POOLING *noun*: When working with multicolored yarn that isn't **self-striping**, there is really no way to know which of its colors is going to wind up where, especially when it is hand painted. Sometimes you get a stripy effect; sometimes you get a mishmash of random colors; and every now and again you get a noticeable, amoeba-shaped section in which every stitch is the same darn color. This is called pooling. It drives some knitters crazy, especially when they are working on **socks** or gloves, and there is a large pool on one item and not on the other. See **twins**. These knitters will **frog** the offending section, remove some yarn, and reknit it, only to discover that instead of solving the problem, they have merely relocated it. Other knitters don't see pooling as a negative and figure that one of the joys of hand-painted yarn is that you get to see the pattern of the yarn evolve as you go, and it is always pretty much a surprise.

If pooling drives you over the edge, the easiest way to make sure it doesn't happen is to alternate using working yarn from two **skeins** of the same **dye lot** as you **knit**. I have also known knitters to cut out a section of a specific color if they see the beginning of a pooled area, but that leaves you with more ends to weave in when the knitting is finished. So perhaps you should consider **Fair Isle** knitting—something in which you can control the color gradations with an iron fist. Or **intarsia**. Or only working with solid colors. Or perhaps the knitters' drugs of choice—wine and chocolate—in whatever ratio makes you feel better about the whole pooling issue.

PROCESS KNITTER *noun*: A knitter who gets his or her primary joy in knitting from the knitting itself, rather than from the acquisition of the **finished object**. You might be a process knitter if your basket is full of **WIPs**, and that doesn't bother you at all; you have **knit** an afghan that is large enough to be used as emergency shelter by your entire family; or you have knit a stack of **swatches** that is taller than you are, but you haven't started any of the actual projects you have swatched. It is the movement that matters, the feel of the yarn as it runs through your hands, the rhythmic regular clicking of your needles, the challenge of figuring out a complicated stitch pattern. When strangers stop you as you go through your day and ask what you are knitting, you shrug and smile an enigmatic smile. It doesn't matter what you are knitting; it just matters that you are knitting. See also **results knitter**.

PROJECT BAG *noun*: A portable version of your favorite knitting spot at home. Start with a tote bag that you wouldn't be ashamed to be seen with in public. While a Whole Foods bag may be cheap and practical, trust me that people will already be staring at you when you **KIP**, so you don't want to give them any more ammunition to think you are odd. Then, of course, you need the knitting project you are working on and the directions for it. Neat, complete, and ready to roll, right?

Well, you might want to throw in a ball or two of extra yarn, in case you really get going—you don't want to run out and be stuck with nothing to do. Maybe you want a second, easier project in there in case you run into someone you know and haven't seen in forever—you need something sort of mindless, so you can chat and **knit** at the same time. Probably you will want to throw in some notions, like a **stitch marker** or two or twelve, a tape measure, some scissors, and a bunch of **tapestry needles** (because we all know if you put only one in, it is a guarantee that it will get lost). You throw in a sketchbook and pencils in case a genius idea for an afghan crosses your mind—you wouldn't want that to get away. Maybe a stitch dictionary, in case you want to modify either of the projects you are working on. And probably a bottle of water and a snack, because you are carrying the bag anyway, so you might as well be prepared for anything. Now your bag is too small, so you have to go find another one.

You finally get everything in there that you want and/or need, then discover that assembling all of these items has already made you a half an hour late for your appointment, and you can't lift the stupid bag without getting a hernia. So you start over—a small tote bag, a **WIP**, and a faded copy of the pattern. It's all you really need.

PURL *noun*: There are really only two stitches in knitting—the **knit** stitch and the purl stitch. The purl stitch is the one where the yarn is held in front of the work. I have heard tell that there are knitters in the world who dislike purling. I have never understood this idea. To me, purling is half of the arsenal at your disposal—the yin to the knit stitch's yang. There are many ways to get around the no purling thing if you really hate it, but you would be much better served by taking all the clever brain cells that you put in service of your avoidance techniques and just learn to purl, for goodness sake. Tough love here: Get over it. Embrace the purl. Quadruple your available stitch patterns.

QIVIUT *noun*: Qiviut is the designer drug for the hand knitter—wildly expensive, hard to find, and instantly addictive, so that once you have tried it, you will do everything in your power to use it again. Specifically, qiviut is fiber from the under-coat of a musk ox. It is soft as clouds, wonderfully warm, and comes in a range of warm brown colors. I heart qiviut. But I really want to know what obsessed knitter saw a thundering herd of danger-ous animals, felt the very earth quake with their weight as they ran down the plains, and said,

"Damn, I bet their undercoats would make a really cool sweater. Or do you think I could get a **lace weight** out of that?" I pride myself on trying to make everything in my life relate to knitting. But I have to say, I would never have looked at two tons of muskoxen and thought, "Maybe a **Moebius**."

Should you feel emotionally (and financially) strong enough to work with some qiviut today, pick your project carefully. It *does* in fact come in a lace weight, and **lace** is a great way to make expensive yardage go far (see **dollars per hour**). You could also consider qiviut trim or accent areas on a garment made primarily of a cheaper material (like sterling silver).

RESULTS KNITTER *noun*: A knitter who gets his or her primary joy in knitting from the fabulous **finished objects** that result. You know that you are a results knitter if you look upon every holiday as an excuse to wear or bestow knitwear ("Happy Groundhog's Day! Here's a sweater!"), choose the colors in your home décor around your favorite yarn's **colorways**, or haul your knitting with you everywhere, not because having something to do with your hands pleases you, but because every snatched moment of knitting brings you one step closer to finishing yet another project. While you might have several **WIPs** going at once, it is only because you think having multiple projects makes them all get finished faster. You are allergic to frogging and a big fan of **design modifications**. You like to **knit**, but you love to show off your finished items. See also **process knitters**.

REVERSE STOCKINETTE *noun:* This is one of those terms that seems like it should be a lot trickier than it is. Work reverse stockinette in exactly the same manner as **stockinette** (**knit** one row, **purl** one row on straight needles, knit every row in the round), but call the purl side the right side and the knit side the wrong side. That's it. No mystery. A great term to have in your arsenal should you sew a stockinette sweater together inside out, or even accidentally place your hat on your head inside out after a late night knitting.

RIBBING *noun:* Alternating columns of **knit** stitches and **purl** stitches, which makes the work draw in a bit, yet remain stretchy. Ribbing is used at the bottom of many sweaters and sleeves to keep cold air out and at the cuffs of **socks** so they can hug your legs and stay up. Because it is stretchy, ribbing is great for garments that show off your . . . um . . . assets. Which I suppose is also good to know should you wish to keep your assets to yourself and certain select friends and family members—a ribbed sweater is probably not for you. Directions for ribbing tell you how wide the columns should be, for example K1, P1, or K3, P1.

ROVING *noun*: 1. Roving is a length of fiber that has been cleaned and carded but not yet spun into yarn. While most folks buy roving to spin, some knitters have taken to knitting roving as is into thick wonderful items. You might want to at least pretend you are planning on **spinning** the roving in your **stash,** so you can say that it doesn't count toward your **SABLE** quotient because it isn't actually yarn yet. 2. Some manufacturers refer to yarns that do not have a lot of twist to them as roving yarns. Things to beware of when working with roving or roving yarns are that it is possible to break the yarn by pulling too hard, and unplied yarns tend to **pill** quite a bit more than plied yarns. 3. A preamble to adventurous **SEX**—you might do some roving around the store before you pounce on the object of your true desires.

SABLE *phrase*: See **stash acquisition beyond life expectancy**.

SCHEMATIC *noun*: If someone were to draw a stick figure of each piece of the sweater you wanted to make and then write the possible measurements for each size along each edge, that would be a schematic. While pattern book and magazine editors include schematics to help the knitter reproduce the model garment exactly, many of us use these guides to punt when we feel like it. I have a tendency (some might say a problem) to not follow directions with the amount of attention some **designers** might prefer. So when I totally lose track of what I did and when I did it, I know I have at least a prayer of it all working out at the end if I can make my piece match the given measurements.

SEAM *noun*: The part of the knitting project where two pieces are sewn or crocheted together.

SEAM *verb*: The part where you have to join two pieces. No matter how many times you have read the Harry Potter series, the house elves are unlikely to arrive in the night and do your seaming for you. I think the reason so many knitters complain that **finishing** garments takes so long is because they spend twenty hours on the knitting, three years procrastinating about doing the finishing, and then, finally, two or three hours actually seaming things up.

Seaming isn't as hard as it looks and is definitely one of those skills that improves with practice. But I am going to tell you a little secret: There are people out there that you can pay, in dollars or sometimes in fiber, who will do your finishing for you. And they even like it! This is not a myth, unlike the whole house elves thing.

SECOND SOCK SYNDROME (SSS) *noun:* I believe **socks** are the perfect knitting project. They are lightweight and therefore portable; you can use even the most expensive sock yarn available without blowing all of your discretionary income for the year on one project; and you can never have too many, unlike, say, **novelty yarn** scarves. The only real drawback to being a sock knitter is the dreaded Second Sock Syndrome, which sets in when the first sock is finished and you have to make another one exactly like it. This doesn't happen with sweaters or hats—once you have finished the item, you can pretty much count on being able to move on creatively to something else. But you can't wear just one sock. And you surely can't give one sock—people would look at you even more oddly than they already do.

On the first sock, you are really feeling the love. You are trying out new yarn, maybe a new stitch or technique—this is really fun. On the second sock, there are pretty much no surprises, which for some of us (maybe with the short attention spans) takes all the fun out of making it.

Been there, done that, have the sock to prove it. In the never-ending battle of knitter against pattern, we have already won the battle, and there is no suspense left, which makes knitting the second sock feel like it takes about ten times longer than knitting the first one did.

While there is no cure for SSS, there are a few tricks you can use to confuse your brain into thinking you don't have it. One is to **cast on** both socks at the same time, then work a little bit on each one every time you knit. You will wind up finishing both at about the same time, provided of course you don't die of boredom while knitting what is essentially a twelve-inch-long leg. Another is to cast on both socks at the same time on the same needles and work them (one inside the other) at the same time using two separate **skeins** of yarn. Marie Antoinette was said to have used this technique, and it will impress the hell out of your knitter friends (non-knitters won't get why it is so cool). Lastly, if you start when they are young and impressionable, you can convince at least your children that only suckers wear socks that match, and that they are making a fashion statement by going against the sock-wearing grain.

SSS can also occur when you knit gloves or mittens, but for some reason, no one says Second Glove or Mitten Syndrome. I don't know why.

SELF-STRIPING *adjective*: Stripes are fun, and they make even the most simple stitch and garment look impressive. The problem with stripes is that they cause a drastic increase in the number of ends needing to be woven in at the end. Clever dyers have solved this problem by creating self-striping yarns. Yup, the yarn makes stripes all by itself. You don't have to do anything but **knit** away with it. It is like magic.

But there are a few things you need to know about self-striping yarn. First, the greater the number of stitches in your row (the wider the piece you are working on), the narrower the stripe you will get. In some cases, if you are trying to make a really wide shawl, for example, out of self-striping **sock** yarn, you will wreck the math to the point where you won't get stripes at all.

Second, if the piece you are working on varies in width due to **increases** or **decreases**, the height of the stripe will change accordingly. For example, if you decide to knit knee socks and increase or decrease so that the width of the sock at the calf is wider than the width of the sock at the ankle, the stripes will be thinner at the wider part. While the yarn itself is magic, its powers do not extend to adjusting itself to your varying widths.

Third, you can almost never get the color to change exactly where you want. The color change isn't going to line up at the exact beginning or end of any row, and it isn't going to line up over the stitch where it started. If you are compulsive about those sorts of things, you might want to avoid the self-striping yarns. Of course, in this case, you might be one of those strange people who likes to weave in ends, so why take all the fun out of things?

SEX *noun*: See **stash enhancement expedition**.

SHEEP AND WOOL FESTIVALS *noun*: My own little piece of heaven! Sheep and wool festivals are events at which artisans and farmers—pretty much someone from every aspect of the fiber food chain from sheep to shawl—gather for a weekend to show off their wares and entice those of us with low resistance into making a few more purchases.

I love fiber festivals because you can see all sorts of products from artisans and small companies that aren't quite large enough to be wholesaling to your **LYS**. I love them because they attract thousands of knitters and other fiber maniacs who will never look askance at me as I fondle a **skein** of yarn. I love petting the sheep that wants to be a sweater when it grows up, listening to the llamas and alpacas hum, and watching the bunnies hop around. Fiber festivals are the perfect marriage of fiber and snack food, which is way cool (as long as you remember to wash your hands when going back and forth between those two things).

The thing I don't like about sheep and wool festivals? The part where the little lambies aren't considered part of the fiber-bearing aspect but as part of the snack-food aspect. Lambies on a stick or ground up into sausage are not nearly as much fun to imagine as gamboling lambies waiting happily to be shorn.

SHORT ROWS *noun*: Short row shaping is exactly what it sounds like—the knitter works back and forth in rows but doesn't work every stitch in the row. Short rows are common in **sock** patterns and are also the basis of several popular multidirectional scarf patterns. They also can be used in sweaters for bust or waist shaping. Short rows aren't that hard to learn to do; just follow the directions slavishly even if you can't visualize what is going to happen. It will all work out in the end—I promise. In fact, while many knitting teachers recommend reading through all of the directions ahead of time for a project you are considering, for a short row pattern I highly recommend knitting along in blissful ignorance until you get to the short row part. One of my favorite scarf patterns is equal in length to the first draft of *War and Peace* because the **designer** wrote each row out step by step, which I for one thought was very nice of her. The sheer bulk of the pattern is intimidating—but, in fact, after you have done one or two of the short row triangles you can whip right along without reading the pattern because the repeat is so intuitive.

SILK *noun*: Silk is fiber from the cocoon of the silkworm. It is glorious stuff, with a high sheen and soft feel. It is also pretty expensive. It takes a lot of bitty cocoons to make any sort of real yardage. Do you think we could drive the prices down if we all started calling it worm poop instead of silk? Silk is notoriously inelastic (unlike **wool**) and is not usually a great choice for a first project—it shows every itty-bitty variation in your stitches. If the fiber snob in you needs feeding, and you don't knit with machinelike precision, go for the **qiviut**!

SIT-AND-KNIT NIGHT *noun*: A regularly scheduled event at your **LYS** where like-minded fiber folks, sit, chat, munch, cavort, drink out of mysterious bottles wrapped in plain brown paper bags (or maybe that's just my sit-and-knit night), and coincidentally maybe get some knitting done. Even if you have never been to one before, know that they are full of knitters so you will always have something in common with folks you might never have the chance to meet otherwise. There is no struggling to come up with a topic of conversation, even in a room full of strangers, because these people, no matter their ages, careers, or other demographic dividers like to do the same thing you like to do! If you have a tendency to hide in your house for many more hours than is considered normal because you do not like to encounter strangers, I highly recommend a sit-and-knit night adventure. And now that you have read this book, you will be able to kibitz at will, and you will get all the knitting jokes.

SKEIN *noun*: A unit of yarn for sale. Not a uniform measurement, mind you, just the word for that thing the wound yarn comes in. Whether it has seventeen yards or seventeen hundred yards, is cobweb or polar **weight**, is animal fiber or fibers not found in nature, that thing on the shelf is a skein. Well, unless it's a **hank**, but let's not confuse things with the facts.

Most commercial patterns will tell you how many skeins of each yarn the **designer** thinks you need to make the project. This may or may not have anything to do with reality. To be safe, it is always wise to buy one more skein of each yarn than the pattern calls for. This is not a rumor circulated by **LYS** owners to sell more yarn; it is their little way of trying to ensure that you don't run out, and they have to spend twelve hours of their lives tracking one more ball of yak hair in the color "Martian Sunset," **dye lot** number 78367756245158732767658 or you will commit ritual suicide in their classroom areas because you are fifteen yards short. You can always return extra yarn within a reasonable period of time. But who returns yarn?

SLIPPED STITCH *noun*: A stitch that is moved from the left needle to the right needle without being worked. Stitches can be slipped either purl-wise, or knitwise—what the **designer** wants you to do will be spelled out in the pattern. Slipping stitches is used to add texture, to make a color change, or, at the end of a row, to provide a neater edge for **picking up** stitches or **finishing**. If you accidentally slip enough stitches from left to right without knitting, you are going to have an intriguing piece of fabric when all is said and done. Please try to slip stitches responsibly.

SOCKS *noun*: Be very careful when you decide you might want to **knit** your first pair of socks. For some reason that no one can quite put a finger on, sock knitting has some uniquely addictive quali-ties.

Ten—oops—twelve reasons sock knitting is more addictive than crack:

1. It impresses the hell out of non-knitters—especially if you use **DPNs**. Non-knitters tend to think knitting with two needles is impres-sive; wait till they see you manage four or five at a time.

2. You can make a good-quality pair of socks for a yarn cost of less than $10, and even if you buy the most expensive sock yarn on the planet, you still won't max out your credit card. Try that with a sweater.

3. Everyone needs socks. They are the perfect gift for your more puritan family members because they are useful.

4. Socks are the perfect portable project. You can't stick the afghan you are knitting with bulky yarn and size thirty-five needles into your coat pocket, but your sock can go with you anywhere.

5. Socks are a great way to experiment with new stitch patterns in a nonthreatening environment. If you screw up, odds are the **mistake** will be in your shoe or under your pants leg, so no one will see.

6. You can use any of a variety of techniques until you find the one that suits you best— four or five DPNs, two **circular needles**, or **magic loop**.

7. The first time some idiot comes up to you and says, "I don't know what you are doing that for. You can get socks ten for a dollar at the store," you have any number of weapons at

your disposal. You can stab the guy (and it's almost always a guy, isn't it?).

8. Sock yarn doesn't take up much room in your **stash**. If you are space-challenged so far as stash hiding, um, stash storage goes, sock yarn is your friend. You can hide enough yarn for a pair of socks almost anywhere in the house—not so with giant **skeins** of **wool**.

9. Socks will eventually wear out, so you get to go yarn shopping and make more.

10. Socks have endless pattern support. You could make a different pattern for every day of the year and still have a few patterns left over.

11. Conversely, if you find a pattern you love to make that fits you well, you can feel free to repeat it ad nauseam. Your yarn choice will make every pair look different. Striped socks impress non-knitters even more.

12. Once you wear a pair, you will never be able to go back to ten-for-a-dollar socks from the discount store. Hand-knit socks fit like nothing else, especially if you have a hard-to-fit foot.

SPAWN OF SATAN *noun*: See **designer**.

SPINNING *verb*: 1. What your head does when presented with a complicated **lace chart** or **Fair Isle** pattern for the first time. Also a symptom of many choices and a small **yarn budget** at a **local yarn store**. 2. The act of twisting fiber into yarn. Can be accomplished with a drop spindle or any one of a zillion kinds of wheels, but be warned: It is another addictive hobby. Next thing you know, there will be sheep in your backyard and bunnies in your basement. Just be warned.

SPIT SPLICE *noun*: One of the many techniques used by knitters to join the beginning of one ball of yarn to the end of the previous ball of yarn. The prissier among us know it as a **felted join**, but spit splice is just such an evocative term that I would hate to see it go by the wayside. The first thing to know about a spit splice is that it only works on animal fibers—yarns that **felt**. Fray the last two to four inches of the strand you are finishing and the first two to four inches of the new strand and lay one over top of the other in the palm of your hand. Now, spit in your palm (OK, fine, use some warm tap water if you must). It is very important when you do a spit splice that you were *not* just indulging in the knitting drugs of choice (chocolate and wine), because they might leave a stain. This is also not a project to undertake if you were recently indulging your Cheetos jones. In any case, rub your palms together back and forth in a rapid movement, rolling the two ends of the yarn together into one. The three things needed for an item to felt (heat, moisture, and agitation) are all happening here, so the two yarn ends should felt together into one. It will be a bit thicker than the rest of your yarn, so make sure to place your spit splice where the little bitty **gauge** variation won't be noticeable. And you might want to wait until it dries completely before you **knit** past it. Give it a short tug to make sure it will hold together before you move on. See also **Russian join**.

SSS *noun*: See **second sock syndrome**.

STARTITIS *noun*: A tragic disease, thankfully not contagious, that affects both novice and experienced knitters alike. Symptoms include mild fever, a distracted air, and most notably an uncontrollable urge to **cast on** every project which the sufferer has had even the vaguest notion of making. While a mild case of startitis can be over in a day or two, more advanced cases have lasted for months on end.

There is no known cure for startitis, although some concerned family members of victims have reported a lessening of symptoms when the sufferer's exposure to knitting books and patterns, **LYSs**, and Internet pattern libraries, knitting **blogs**, and chat rooms is restricted. In some cases, improvement isn't noted until the knitter's supply of **knitting needles** is cut off completely. Sadly, these treatments leave most patients so darned cranky that in many cases, they aren't worth pursuing.

Because many startitis victims are in denial about their disease due to fear of aggressive treatment, friends and family members can live with a sufferer for weeks before they realize that the virus has worsened. Don't let your friends suffer from startitis in silence. Be on the lookout for a drastic increase in visible **WIPs**, a constant low mumbling while the knitter tries to sort out which of the eighteen hundred patterns she has in progress she is supposed to be working on now, and the predilection of WIPs to spring out of hiding places where no knitting ought to be. Should you see these symptoms, don't be afraid to speak up, even though the knitter is armed with a pile of pointy sticks. Acknowledgment of the problem is the first step toward outwitting this crafty disease.

STASH *noun*: The yarn that will eventually be knitted up. The key word here is *eventually*. Stash yarn never expires and has an infinite shelf life, so the amount of time between purchase and use can span decades. Because some stash hangs around for a long time before the perfect project is found for it, stash has a tendency to grow . . . and grow . . . and grow, spreading as rapidly as a computer virus, especially when there is a sale or a **sheep and wool festival**. Stash doesn't have to be used to be appreciated; it is perfectly normal to take it out and examine it from time to time, often on the pretext of using some of it, but sometimes just because. Should there be a worldwide **wool** blight, the dedicated knitter won't run out of projects for years. In fact, I suspect if doomsday comes, **merino** may be used as currency during the end of days. See also **SEX** and **SABLE**.

STASH ACQUISITION BEYOND LIFE EXPECTANCY (SABLE) *phrase*: As in, she who dies with the biggest **stash** wins. Also as in,

"Watch the checkbook balance. She's going SABLE!" I personally don't think there is any such thing as SABLE. I just need to live a really long time to get to all the yarny goodness that is in the closet . . . and the bottom drawer of the dresser . . . and the cedar chest . . . and the trunk of the car . . .

STASH ENHANCEMENT EXPEDITIONS (SEX)

noun: In other words, a road trip with yarn.

There are all kinds of SEX: cheap SEX (there is a sale at a chain store); casual SEX (I'm not sure why I am doing this, but it feels too good to pass up); even committed SEX (I am going to the **LYS** at 5:45 on Friday afternoon and buy the yarn I need for a specific project and nothing else). And if you have never had group SEX with the members of your knitting guild or even friends and family members, you just don't know what you are missing.

Some people like to take precautions before SEX (I will only take one credit card and no checks so I can't spend too much money), and, of course, some just go hog wild and throw caution to the wind. Only you can decide for yourself how much SEX is too much SEX.

A well-planned SEX drive will include more than one stop to maximize the potential for all involved to find something that will float their boats, so to speak. It will also include a lunch or coffee break to refresh and refuel for further activities—the body needs sustenance for prolonged bouts of SEX.

Many knitters feel a morning-after letdown after a whole day of SEX. This is usually cured by having a good wallow in all of the lovely balls of yarn you bought, provided of course you haven't had to hide them already from potentially angry family members. ("You spent how much on what? What about all that other yarn in the closet?") And if the depression is too great, perhaps it is time to begin planning your next expedition. After all, with SEX, anticipation greatly adds to the pleasure.

STEEKS *noun*: A process, often used in **Fair Isle** knitting, in which the knitter spends a zillion hours carefully knitting a multicolored sweater in the round, then cuts it up with very sharp scissors. I am not kidding, this is actually what happens: You **knit** a beautiful sweater and then cut it up.

Why this is a good idea—at least on paper: Working with several colors of yarn back and forth in rows can be a pain in the rear. You can see what you are doing much more easily when working in the round. All you have to manage are knit stitches, and the yarn is always traveling in the same direction. However, if you are making a cardigan or want any of the basics like armholes or neck openings, **knitting in the round** doesn't really work forever. So you knit what looks like a giant tube and then cut the openings where you need them. After your openings are secured, you can sew in your sleeves and **pick up** stitches for the neck bands and collar bands.

This is not as reckless as it sounds. Knitters experienced in this technique mark the cutting lines by knitting a different pattern so they know exactly where to cut. They use yarns that tend to stick to each other and not fray (like Shetland **wool**), or reinforce the openings with rows of sewing or **crochet**. They check and double-check their measurements, and then cut away.

I am told that cutting steeks is a liberating moment—a way to connect with traditional knitters of the past, a way to get an undeniably beautiful garment. I am here to tell you that the mere thought of putting sharp scissors to knitted color work makes me queasy. I have never cut steeks. I have never gone bungee jumping either. I think the likelihood that I will try either is roughly the same—slim to none.

STOCKINETTE STITCH *noun:* Stockinette stitch is one of the basics—it has a smooth side (the right side) and a bumpy side (the wrong side). When working back and forth in rows, alternate **knit** rows (right side) with **purl** rows (wrong side. When working in the round, knit every row. There are knitters who love to just cruise along knitting stockinette stitch in a solid color—mindless knitting to keep their hands busy while their brains are puzzling over other problems (like who is going to implode on *Project Runway* this week?) or taking a much-needed vacation. I am not one of those knitters—give me interest, or at least an interesting yarn, or give me death (death being a mile of one-color **garter stitch**).

STRESS KNITTING *verb:* When the going gets tough, the tough get knitting.

"I can't believe you would rather **knit** than look at this Doppler scan," the vascular surgeon said as he ran the scanner over my husband's leg. After having successfully picked out the femoral artery on the screen at the doctor's direction by looking for a silhouette of Mickey Mouse, I had lost interest in the gray blur on the screen and was trying to drown out the white noise in my head with the busy clicking of my needles. Did my husband have a post-operative blood clot? Would it move to his heart or his brain and kill him? Would it hurt? Would I be a widow, my child fatherless? Was there food in the house? Would I make it back to school in time to pick up my daughter? Who would get her if I couldn't? The faster the questions spun around my head, the faster the needles went. It isn't that I didn't want to look at the Doppler scan as much as I couldn't imagine what would happen to my brain if I dared to put those needles down. I clung to that poncho for my daughter like I was an astronaut and the blue fuzzy yarn was the last tether to the mother ship. Yes, he had a clot, but there was no immediate risk, so I could take him home. I stuffed the yarn in the bag and jingled my car keys, anxious to be on my way.

A few days later we were back at the surgeon's. The blue poncho was finished, and I had started a pair of black and gray **cashmere** fingerless mitts. "What happened to the blue stuff?" asked the doctor. "Finished," I replied. "Really?" he asked. "I have never seen anyone knit like you." He watched me make a few stitches, mesmerized, then shook it off and went on with his work.

I was just about to finish the second glove when Dr. M took me inside his office to explain that my husband was indeed at a risky stage, and even though it was two days before Christmas, he had to go directly to the nearest hospital for intravenous medication. As he looked from my panicked expression to the full-to-bursting knitting bag on my lap, he smiled gently. "Perhaps you should consider starting a blanket," he said.

In front of a new and admiring audience at the hospital, I started (and finished) a pink, flower-shaped washcloth out of fluffy cotton yarn. My husband joked that if I ran out of things to make, he had scouted a yarn store not far down the road that I could slip out to for another fix. At least I think he was joking. On Christmas Eve I brought him home from the hospital and ran around like a crazy person hunting down his hard-to-find meds and some food, for the cupboard was bare. On Christmas Day, enjoying a brief respite from both medical and holiday madness, I **cast on** the blanket.

129

When the blanket got too big to carry around, I started a pair of red **wool socks**. Socks are the perfect stress knitting—they are light and portable and take a good long time to finish. A nurse I had never seen before looked over my shoulder in delight—she was a knitter, too, but had never made socks. I turned the first heel that afternoon, finished the first sock, and started the second as the visits added up. The nurse always checked my sock progress as she checked the levels of the medicine thinning my husband's blood. The socks gave way to a shrug, a shawl, a bunch of items for my charity basket, and another blue poncho for my daughter's best friend's birthday party. I craved the feel of the wool as it passed through my hands and marked the days of my husband's illness with the growing pile of knitwear I left in my wake. Whenever I put the needles down, the questions popped up again: Did I pay the water bill? Had I called my mother? Did I miss a deadline?

It wasn't mindful knitting I craved but mindless knitting—knitting that occupied enough of my brain to direct its hyperactivity but wasn't so challenging that I couldn't drag it around with me. More socks, more mitts, a few scarves, and a pair of slippers. Packages shipped to Vermont,

Indiana, and Mongolia—hand knits wrapped for future giving.

Some months later, the urgency abated, both in my knitting and in my husband's medical needs. He was learning to put down his crutches, and I my needles. Except I won't ever really put them down for good. I'll just replace my clutching, hamster-on-a-wheel, complete-inability-to-slow-down knitting with some calmer, happier, maybe even more challenging knitting.

What's on the needles now? A shawl and a pair of socks—one project for home and one to drag to my daughter's dance class and the knitting store's social events. I don't miss the frantic quality of the work that came before, although my daughter regrets that she has new things to show off at school a little less frequently. I am happy that I made a big dent in my **stash**, although if I am being completely honest I need to point out that the stress knitting was accompanied on some days by some stress yarn shopping. You think knitting is cheaper than therapy? Not if you buy the good stuff!

The doctor, on the rare days that I see him now, asks what I am knitting as soon as he walks into the room. And I think the nurse may have to try a pair of socks.

SUBSTITUTION, YARN *noun*: You open up the newest knitting book on the shelf of the **LYS** and see the sweater of your dreams. It is a glorious pattern, and it would flatter you like nothing else, but it is made of yarn from some nearly endangered species at the outer reaches of the planet, which makes it cost so much per **skein** that you would have to take out a second mortgage to buy enough for a long-sleeved sweater. Time for some well-thought-out subbing.

The key to happy subbing is the well-thought-out part. You need to think about **gauge**, **weight**, fiber content, yardage, and color. Gauge and yardage are the big kahunas here. You can't easily substitute **sock** yarn for chunky, and if you buy fifteen skeins of yarn because the pattern said so, but you are using yarn that comes in sixty-five-yard skeins and the designer was using yarn that came in two-hundred-yard skeins, you are going to have a big problem when you run out.

Let the happy denizens of your LYS help you if they can. They have a good breadth of knowledge about the yarn used in the pattern books and may have already helped another customer substitute successfully. But expect to do a gauge **swatch**—it really is the best way to make sure you have made an accurate substitution.

SUPERWASH *adjective*: When I first saw this on a **label**, I dreamed that superwash **wool** meant it would wash itself ("Look, up in the sky—it's a bird, it's a plane, it's a self-cleaning afghan. Woohoo!") and sadly that is not quite the case. The good news is that superwash wool has been chemically treated to make it easy to wash and dry—especially handy for things that need to be cleaned often, like **socks** or toddler garments. The most important thing to remember about superwash is that it does not **felt**. This could be a good thing or a bad thing, depending on your project.

SWATCH *noun*: A small sample, at least four inches square, made to measure **gauge**. No one wants to **knit** swatches. Everyone wants to jump right in and **cast on** the project. To solve this problem I propose we eliminate the name swatch and tell folks they are knitting something else entirely. Squares for an afghan, doll blankets, baby washcloths, coasters, bookmarks, whatever—just not swatches. That way we can trick ourselves into thinking we are making project progress rather than wasting prime knitting time.

SWIFT, UMBRELLA *noun*: If you want to wind yarn from **hanks** into balls more swiftly, you should consider purchasing a swift. A swift is a wood or metal tool that clamps onto your worktable and has a tall vertical shaft, surrounded by a circular lattice that is adjustable to various widths. The mechanism used to do the adjusting resembles the workings of an umbrella, thus the name. Expand the lattice until it just fits inside your untwisted hank of yarn, find the end and run it to the **ball winder**, and gently turn the swift as you wind your yarn, letting the strand unwind smoothly from the hank. Warning: Once you acquire an umbrella swift and especially if you got a ball winder at the same time, you will feel a burning desire to find and wind up every hank of yarn in your **stash**, just because it is so much fun and provides a great sense of instant gratification. Schedule your life accordingly.

If you do not have a swift, you can substitute a chair back or the outspread hands of your significant other. I highly recommend the latter form of torture—it provides great impetus for the person in question to go out and buy you a swift of your very own.

TELEVISION *noun*: Background noise for knitters. You can lounge in front of the boob tube and watch any old trashy television show without guilt because while other folks are wasting brain cells watching this drivel, you are actually making great use of this time by creating art. It is a wonderful way to indulge you mindless TV jones and retain the moral high ground all at the same time.

Ten ways to know when a knitter has committed a crime, or, "Clearly I watch too many police procedurals on television when I am power knitting," with apologies to author Maggie Sefton:

1. Police arrive at the scene of a reported break-in to discover that while no electronics or jewels are missing, there is a large empty closet and a sobbing woman wearing a hand-knit sweater.

2. The cause of death was nine thousand very small 2.5 mm puncture wounds.

3. The bank was robbed of small bills, and the perpetrator left behind a piece of scrap paper with the word "Rhinebeck" scribbled on it.

4. The escapees made it out the window with a ladder made of **I-cord** cleverly knitted with week-old spaghetti on two double-pointed toothbrushes.

5. They also blended into the general public having dyed their prison duds with Kool-Aid saved from the previous months' lunches one sip at a time.

6. There were no footprints left at the scene (the perpetrators must have worn hand-knit **socks**), but the CSIs were deluged with unlikely fiber traces. ("Buffalo, Bob? There are no buffalo in Boca Raton!")

7. The potential witness was bound to her chair, not with duct tape, but with hundreds of yards of (durable yet inexpensive) dishcloth cotton.
8. And her blindfold was hand-knit **cashmere**—any lesser fiber would be too itchy to wear next to the skin.
9. White wine and chocolate stains were found at the scene.
10. Two dark getaway llamas were spotted grazing nearby at the time of the incident.

Actually this list is even sillier than it sounds because we all know that knitters are too nice to commit crimes—or at least too smart to get caught.

TENSION *noun*: 1. What you feel in an **LYS** when you have $500 worth of wants and $50 worth of disposable income. 2. **Gauge** if you are European or aspire to the aristocracy.

THERAPY, KNITTING IS BETTER THAN *phrase*: We have all heard that knitting is cheaper than therapy. But the fact of the matter is, if your tastes run toward hand-paint, **cashmere**, or hand-painted cashmere, (or, of course, if you found a cut-rate therapist), this isn't really true. And I have never bought the "best things in life are free" philosophy, because frankly, I have never run across a reliable supply of free **sock** yarn, and we all know that sock yarn is one of the best things in life. But, cost be damned, knitting is *better* than therapy—and here are ten of the many reasons why:

1. Knitting is much more portable than a therapist. You can't stuff your counselor in a tote bag and take her with you whenever you think you might feel stressed.

2. Knitting doesn't charge by the fifty-minute hour.

3. Knitting is available 24/7. You will never have to add to your general angst by wondering if your knitting really hates you because you woke it up at three in the morning. It doesn't.

4. Knitting does not take the month of August off.

5. You do not have to leave your house to **knit**, although you can if you need a change of scenery.

6. People stare at you less if you knit in public than if you vent in public. They might still

stare, but it could be out of genuine interest rather than mild fright.

7. The medications associated with knitting (chocolate and white wine) are available without a prescription.

8. When the knitting is over, there is something to hold in your hands. Not only do you feel better, but you look fabulous.

9. The knitting community is a lot more fun than the therapeutic community. **Sit-and-knit nights** tend to be much looser than group therapy and can provide much the same stress relief.

10. **Stash**—'nough said.

The only real downside to knitting instead of therapy is that health insurance doesn't tend to cover yarn. But we can always hope that some enlightened actuary somewhere will see the correlation between knitting and mental health and lobby for **merino** coverage. It could happen.

THROWING *verb*: 1. A common term for **English knitting**, because the English knitter throws the working yarn around the needle rather than **picking** it with the needle tip as in **Continental knitting**.

2. What the knitter will be doing to her **novelty yarn** once the novelty has worn off—about twenty minutes into the project.

TINK *verb*: Un-Knit. Achieved by pulling the working yarn out one stitch at a time and transferring the stitches back from the right needle to the left, one by one. Derived from **knit** spelled backward. If you have made a **mistake** in the earlier part of a row you are working on, you may have to tink back a few stitches to fix the mistake. If the mistake you have made can't be considered a **design modification** and is farther back than the row you are working on, it may be time for a visit to the **frog pond**.

Sadly, the whole backward word thing doesn't really work anywhere else in knitting—we don't lrup when we rip out **purl** stitches, or hsinif when we undo a **seam** for the three hundredth time because it is crooked. I suspect it is a pronunciation issue. God only knows what kind of obscenities would come out of our mouths if we used hsats when we did a little de-stashing.

TOO PRETTY TO USE *phrase*: An all-purpose catchphrase used by the recipient of a hand-knitted gift that loosely translated means, "This is going into the **black hole** in the back of the closet and will never see the light of day again." There are several sub meanings, however. Here are the most common.

1. "It really *is* too pretty to use." The recipient loves the gift, is knocked out that you went to the trouble to create it for her, and is terrified that somehow if she uses the gift, she will screw it up in some horrible way. Explain gently to this person that knitted items don't like to languish on closet shelves, and that you have perfect faith that they can handle the responsibility of the perfect gift. If that doesn't work, explain that it can be a fine thing if they lose that scarf on the subway, because then you get to go yarn shopping without guilt so you can make another one!

2. "I would no more wear a hand-knitted item than I would stick a fork in my eye, but I understand that for some strange reason this is important to you so I will try really hard not to say that out loud." While this one may sting in the short term, in the long term this is good information to have. You won't waste valuable knitting time on folks who can't

141

appreciate a hand-knitted gift, and if you never again **knit** something for this guy, he won't mind. The only real downside is that you kind of have to let go of worrying about the fate of the item you already made. Perhaps you can steal it back when you visit next—it isn't like it will ever be missed.

3. "I love it, but I don't want to take care of it." Many people raised in the land of wash and wear and dry cleaners who pick up and deliver are terrified when faced with taking care of a hand knit. So they figure if they don't use it, they won't ever have to wash it. A great way around this is to start the person off with easy-care fibers and to attach a care tag to the gift before you give it.

4. "I am saving it for the right occasion." OK, maybe this one is only my family (although I suspect not), but there is always one family member who loves the gift they got so much that they put it away for a special occasion, which never seems to come. This is an especially common trait in those who lived through or had parents who lived through the Great Depression. It is hard to get around this one without being a nag—but know that if

this recipient hated the gift, he or she would probably use it until it was a rag!

There is no real way to knit for your family and friends and get through life without hearing "It's too pretty to use" at least once. Forewarned is forearmed. If it really bothers you, consider picking up charity knitting. No one who was cold ever worried about saving a warm garment for "best."

TWINS, FRATERNAL OR IDENTICAL *noun*: When one has to make two of something in order to use them—**socks**, gloves, mittens, etc.—many knitters spend a great deal of effort trying to make sure that both items look exactly the same, that they are identical twins. This is not so hard to do with solid-colored yarns but is quite a feat when using **self-striping** or variegated yarns.

Sometimes, no matter how careful you are, your two halves of a whole pair wind up looking more like cousins. It could be an error on your part, or more likely the fact that each **skein** of yarn is going to behave slightly differently. So if anyone comments that your socks don't match when you know you used the same **colorway** for each one, just tell the commenter that your socks are fraternal rather than identical twins.

UFO *noun*: See **unfinished object**.

UNFINISHED OBJECT (UFO) *noun*: Although
a knitting project could easily be turned into a
flying object when the frustrated knitter uncere-
moniously hurls it across the room toward the
deepest recesses of the **frog pond,** the more common definition for the UFO acronym in knitting
is unfinished object. What is the difference between
UFO and **WIP**? The P. In other words a work in
progress usually has some forward movement

(progress) happening, while a UFO is more like the throw that I started for my mother in 1992 and last worked on in the last millennium. Seriously.

Although there is no scientific proof to support this, it is claimed by some that UFOs breed and multiply in the darkness, which is their preferred habitat. They also have a tendency to fade quickly from the memory of the knitter who created them—helping to ensure that they live out their lives in peace and tranquility.

Occasionally an intrepid knitter will go on an expedition to reclaim these projects, only to discover that she is severely outnumbered. While some knitters retreat in the face of almost overwhelming odds, the braver amongst us banish these creatures to the frog pond, almost always reclaiming dozens of **knitting needles** and hundreds of dollars worth of books and patterns in the process.

Many UFOs don't require any additional knitting at all. They have retreated into inactivity due to the knitter's avoidance of the **finishing** process.

WEAVING IN ENDS *verb*: The boring part of **fin-ishing** any knitting project. Any project has ends to weave in—at the beginning and the end of each piece, for example—but some projects, espe-cially those with a lot of color changes, have many ends to weave in. The process can be made easier by making sure you plan for it. Every time you cut a yarn, make sure you leave a long enough tail to comfortably work with. In some instances, I leave really long tails, knowing that I can use that yarn to sew up a **seam**, too. Weave in the end by working it deep into the back of the work or the inside of a finished seam. You don't want the ends to pull out with wear or cleaning and have to be woven in again. Once was bad enough.

WEIGHT *noun*: 1. What you will put on by doing nothing but sitting in your chair knitting fever-ishly to the exclusion of all other activity. 2. The yarn's thickness, not the weight of the **skein** (which is usually 1.75 ounces/50grams or 3.5 ounces/100grams). The Craft Yarn Council of America has a series of numbered yarn designa-tions from 1 (dental floss for fairies) to 6 (rope with which to climb Mount Everest), but com-monly used weight names from thinnest to thick-est are: **lace weight** or cobweb; fingering, baby, or **sock**; dk or sport; worsted or aran; and bulky, chunky, or polar weight.

WHISPERER, KNITTING *noun*: Knitters joke about being able to recognize other knitters they haven't met by the **DPNs** poking out of their pockets or the knitted garments that they wear, but I believe there are those among us that sort of radiate knitterly vibes that only other knitters can pick up on. I believe I am one of those people.

If you are looking for someone to help you in an **LYS** and you see me, you think I work there, even if I have my coat and purse with me. If I am shopping at a yarn sale, people come up to me and ask my opinion about the purchases they are considering: Is the yarn nice? Do they have enough of it for a long-sleeved sweater? Is it a good price? I have a wonderful neighbor who, on the night we met, asked me to fix a problem she was having on the leg of a knitted soaker. Actually, the fact that she had a problem with her knitting is the reason we met in the first place—she had heard from others on the block that I could fix her knitting and stopped by to introduce herself, knitting in hand. Even when I am not **KIP**ing, I seem to have a sign flashing on my forehead that says: "Knitter, and not only a knitter, but the type of obsessed knitter that will stop whatever she is doing without hesitation to talk yarn with you or fix your projects." OK, it's a really big sign . . .

But I am not the only one. There is bound to be a knitting whisperer at your local **knit** night, and I know you know who she is. She is the one who never gets her own knitting done because she is too busy helping everyone else with theirs. She is the one whose knitting bag is bulging at the

seams and always, like Mary Poppins, seems to have just exactly whatever it is that you think you need at her immediate disposal. If it turns out you were wrong about what you needed, she has the right thing in there, too. She can diagnose a knitting aberration from twenty paces, knows fifteen ways to **cast on**, and can converse intelligently on the technical merits of the yarn made from every species of fiber-bearing animal on the planet. And she is pleasant, too. Her aim is to make conversation, have a good time, and help other knitters, never to show off what she knows or how she knows it. Cultivate the acquaintance of one of these folks should you find one. You never know when you will need her special knowledge to help you out of a jam.

WIP *noun*: See **work in progress**.

WOOL *noun*: A gateway drug, it is the fiber from a sheep. There are all sorts of **labels** that can come before the word wool: words like **superwash** refer to how the yarn was treated; words like **merino** or Leicester to the breeds of sheep whose fleece make up the yarn; words like **boucle** to how the yarn was made.

WORK IN PROGRESS (WIP) *noun*: Progress being in the mind of the beholder, of course. Many of us have location-specific WIPs: one in the car, one in the tote bag for our brushes with mass transit or dentists' waiting rooms, one in the living room, one by the bed—a WIP for wherever we are that might offer up some knitting time, so that we are never caught without a project. I tend to organize my WIPs according to brain cells required while working on them. I have one project that requires my full attention at the same time that I have one or two others that I can work on while watching television, listening to my family bicker and pretending to pay attention, or while comatose. See also **UFO**, **startitis**.

YARN BUDGET *noun*: An oxymoron. Do we budget the air we breathe, the sun we bask in, the water we drink? No, we don't. And for some of us, good yarn is as important as any of those things. Should we try to consider things like paying the rent or the electric bill when we are shopping for yarn? I suppose, if only so that we have some place to **knit** and enough light to see by. However, one can be creative with the overall budget in order to spend more money on yarn.

Take food, for example. Granted one needs to consume some calories to have enough energy to manipulate the needles, but carefully planning your eating habits around visiting stores that offer free samples, or the work schedule of your colleague who always brings great food but forgets it in the refrigerator, or even the odd blind date can prevent you from ever having to go food shopping. And clothing? If you focus your knitting efforts on clothing, all you need to budget for is the odd set of underwear every few years. Just be sure not to cut back on things like Internet connections (how else can you keep up with the 1,200 knit **blogs** you have bookmarked?) or cable **television** (you need something to keep you occupied when you are knitting a never-ending **stockinette stitch** sweater).

YARN CAKES *noun*: I have no idea who originated this term, but it is used by a lot of folks to refer to the balls of yarn that come off of a **ball winder**. They are flat on each side and easy to store, and I guess saying "yarn cake" is a lot easier than saying "yarn that started out in a **hank** but has now been wound on a ball winder." But if we are calling things names based on what they look like, I would much prefer "yarn hockey puck." I wonder if it will catch on?

YARN OVER *noun*: 1. A deliberate **increase** made by looping the working yarn over the right-hand needle, which will give you one more stitch to work on the following row. Yarn overs are very common in **lace** knitting, because they leave a small hole, lending to the overall airy, fairy-ness of lace work. They are also handy when making **buttonholes**. 2. An accidental increase made by unknowingly running the working yarn over the right-hand needle, often made by beginners when changing from **knit** to **purl** or vice versa in the same row. There is no easy way to get rid of an unwanted yarn over, and you can only really call it a **design modification** if there is a way to convince folks that you needed a buttonhole in the center back of your sweater. **Tink** if you can, or it's off to the **frog pond**.

YARN PORN *noun*: A term used on a **knit blog** when talking about beautiful photography of fabulous yarn. The term is usually purposely misspelled as yarn pron or yarn pr0n to keep from attracting folks who are looking for sex sites. Imagine the poor sod who does a search on "porn" and ends up looking at close-up shots of hand-painted **alpaca**. Better yet, let's don't imagine someone who searches for porn and doesn't mean yarn.